Shadows On My Mind

Shadows on my mind:

A Psychologist Explores Reincarnation and PSI

by

Marie Gates

ISBN: 1-58500-997-0

Please send all correspondence with the author to the following address. Additional copies of *SHADOWS ON MY MIND* may be ordered for $15.00, which includes postage.

Marie Gates
P.O. Box 183166
Shelby Twp., MI 48318-3166

About the Book

Marie Gates may be the only woman in America with her own death certificate. She obtained it in the fall of 1979 while researching her past life as Amanda Randall, a stenographer in depression-era New England. Ms. Gates uncovered Amanda's name and city in hypnotic regressions. On a visit to the area she found Amanda's daughter, Amanda Jones. Mrs. Jones described her mother's death, in a Catholic hospital, the way Ms. Gates had remembered it from infancy. Ms. Gates was not a firm believer in reincarnation, but Amanda Randall had died exactly three months before her own birth, and she has no other explanation for her earliest memory. Ms. Gates learned about similarities between Amanda Randall and herself and realized how the previous life has affected her. *SHADOWS ON MY MIND* compares the past-life and present personalities. On the way to self discovery, Ms. Gates experienced synchronicity and psychic events. Her research provides a framework for understanding them, and enriches the book.

To Martha, and in memory of Michael,

who made this book possible.

CONTENTS

Introduction

The following story is true, but names have been changed to protect the privacy of individuals.

Hypnosis was used to uncover information in this book. I do not recommend casual experimentation with it as this may bring forth, or worsen, emotional issues. A professional hypnotist should be consulted for past-life regression, as a person under hypnosis can become fearful or agitated and may require a skilled person to calm her. However, there is no guarantee this will eliminate difficulties.

I worked with an experienced hypnotist, yet after past-life regression I was confused about my identity. At times I felt fragmented, as if part of me were in twentieth century America but another portion of myself was in the world of a past life. For a time I became unbalanced, preferring the alternate life, wishing I could leave this one. Fortunately, a new job enabled me to ground myself in reality.

Consultation with a psychic or healer may also yield past life information. As the material comes from the practitioner this method is less risky for the seeker. To find a reputable hypnotist, psychic, or healer I recommend consulting a local metaphysical society.

If verification is sought, the names of people, as well as when and where they lived, is essential. Records of births, marriages, and deaths may be obtained from cities and counties. Consult libraries and historical societies for old newspapers and additional resources, which may include obituaries and other information. Some libraries carry U.S. Census records, which list the ages and sexes of persons living in a household, helpful in placing children. For past lives in the twentieth century, city directories may aid in finding persons who knew, or were related to, a past-life identity. The internet can also be a good source for locating people.

Verily, verily, I say unto thee, except a man be born again,

he cannot see the kingdom of God.

_____

St. John: Chapter 3, Verse 3

Chapter One

Early Mysteries in My Life

My earliest memory was my death in a Catholic hospital. The room was plain, and I don't recall any other patients. Two nuns in their white habits moved like shadows in the background. One carried linens, but from my bed I couldn't see what the other was doing. Only my daughter was attending me; no one else was near.

On that February morning Amanda wore a scarf and a long wool coat. I sensed she was upset. Maybe she was afraid her boss would be angry if she were late for work again. She hovered around my bed, soothing me in soft tones, and I was glad to have her there.

I thought I might be dying, but I didn't want to worry Amanda. She had been a wonderful daughter, so good to Jake and me. I was tired, very tired. Life had been hard. With the ulcer and migraines I should have quit work sooner. But I had to help put food on the table and pay the rent. Jake had been out of work, and the DPW didn't pay much.

Never mind, I was proud of my children, and Jake had been a good husband. In better times . . .

When I think about the death scene now I imagine Amanda reviewing her life, giving thanks for the good things, acknowledging the difficulty of the Depression, and regretting she was unable to spend more time with her children.

I suppose she thought of her daughter's upcoming wedding, likely in the spring of that year, 1946. How beautiful Amanda's dark tresses and tanned skin would look against the whiteness of her veil and dress. Would she carry a bouquet of sweet-smelling roses?

Pride would glimmer in Jake's eyes as he escorted her down the aisle to the sound of the organ at the Congregational church. Not the Catholic church, as he would have preferred, but that of his soon to be son-in-law. Jake was not one to harbor grudges. He would no more let religious differences spoil his daughter's wedding than he had let them sour his marriage.

Amanda and her sisters Marie and Anna would weep in their pews, blotting their tears with embroidered handkerchieves. Their little Amanda would shortly become Lyle's wife and go to live with him. How empty the house would feel without her.

Amanda hoped Jim, her only other child, would be able to attend the spring wedding. He had been recently released from the army, and two days before he had arrived from California. She had worked hard to get the house in order for his homecoming, but only hours after Amanda had welcomed him the bleeding had started and an ambulance had rushed her to the hospital.

Jim was a handsome man now, tall and strong, not like the sickly child she had worried over. He was her reason for living, and when he was drafted she had been heartbroken. Now Jim was home, and she lay frustrated in the hospital. Amanda wanted to sneak out, but she knew better.

It was her ulcer. Why did it bleed now, when she longed to be with her son? Perhaps Amanda bit her lip to keep back the tears as a frightening thought entered her mind. What if she didn't get well? She had received a lot of blood, thanks to her daughter's co-workers, but she wasn't recovering. She was weak, her stomach still pained, and she kept passing blood. How long could her body withstand the strain?

No. She couldn't die. Not without seeing her grandchildren. She imagined Amanda would have a boy and a girl, as she herself had borne. A blue-eyed boy like Jim and a dark-haired girl like Amanda and herself, a girl who would get golden in summer. She couldn't miss the scampering of little feet on the beach or the giggles while sitting on Santa's lap. No. Life wouldn't be that cruel to her.

2

Amanda might have prayed to a God she hoped would listen to her. Would he forgive her for avoiding church, for attending only the special events where her children were involved? I imagine she believed in a merciful God, one who understood and forgave, not a rigid, vengeful entity who would punish her for her private faith. At death she was at peace with herself. I remember her last moments as if they were yesterday:

Death came quickly, shocking both my daughter and me.

Suddenly I couldn't breathe. I gasped for air. Every breath was an effort. Then I couldn't inhale. I felt hot all over, suffocating. Was I dying? I didn't want to die, but my body was betraying me. I felt confined and wanted to burst out of my skin. What was the matter? "Help!" I silently screamed, but it was no use. "I suppose this is it," was my last thought as I slipped away. I remember nothing after that.

Before I learned to talk images of the dying woman, her daughter, and the nuns were in my mind, challenging me to make sense of them. Who were they? Where did they come from? Why was this my first memory? I had no answers to these questions until I was thirty-three years old. Then I went through a change which gave me insight into the unknown. A hypnotist helped me recall Amanda's name and city, and with a little effort I located her daughter, Amanda Jones, who revealed the circumstances of her mother's death:

"I was bitter about it for a long time," she said. "If she had had better care it wouldn't have happened. She had an ulcer, but the doctors in those days..."

"Where did she die?"

"She was at St. John's Hospital for two days. The nuns did what they could, but the ulcer had ruptured. She died Tuesday morning at six o'clock."

When Amanda mentioned nuns I became excited. "That's amazing! When I was a little girl I saw myself as an old woman dying in a hospital bed with my daughter and nuns in the room. Were you with your mother when she died?"

"I held her hand."

"Were you wearing a scarf?"

"I may have been," she said softly.

I shivered, and goosebumps erupted on my arms. Had I found the old woman?

At that point I didn't believe in past lives; the hypnotic regressions were an attempt to understand a mysterious dream, a dream which haunted me day and night. However, when I reviewed my life some experiences seemed to support reincarnation.

I was born in Michigan just after World War II., one of the first of the baby boom generation. My parents had tried to have a child for five years, so I was special. Long before my birth they had chosen a name for a daughter: Mary Ann. The name has a long history in my family. My mother's first name is Mary, and so was her mother's and maternal grandmother's. My father's mother was named Anna, as was his paternal grandmother. Dad's great-aunt, who had died young, had been called Maria Anna.

I was a strawberry blonde baby, and when my parents took me out in the buggy strangers admired my hair. They couldn't see the black streak down the back, an unusual birthmark which turned to gray as I grew.

When I was almost two my father moved us to his parents' nearly centennial dairy farm. As a child I was proud only the Indians had made their home on the land before us. We had lived in a house about five miles away, near a small town. Mom didn't want to move into the farmhouse with her in-laws, so my parents had our small house moved next door to Grandma and Grandpa.

Not long after we moved Sandy was born. She had brown hair. I wouldn't give up my red hair for anything, but dark hair seemed prettier, and in the summer Sandy tanned.

One day when I was four I looked into the mirror to check my hair, but a lot more was going on inside. As I looked at myself I thought, "I am really alive." I could barely believe it. In the back of my mind was the dying woman. Scary. The old lady was scary. I felt confused. Who was the old woman, and why did I think I was her? How could I be a little girl when a short time ago I had been an old woman?

I asked my mother, and she said I must have dreamed of the old lady. I half believed her because I didn't understand what was in my head. I was glad she didn't punish me for what some people would think was lying. Maybe she was easy on me because of the things that had happened in her life. Her grandmother could "see" things others couldn't, and when she learned Mom could too she warned her young granddaughter not to work at it. She might not like what she found. When Mom's father died she saw a vapor rise from his body, and his favorite clock stopped, never to work again. Sometimes Mom's dreams came true.

My dad didn't pay much attention to my "dream", but he got angry after he wrote our last name on a piece of paper. **Pace** had only four letters and looked strange to me. "That isn't my name," I said in a loud voice. "Mine is longer."

"It's our name," he told me. When I said it wasn't again he gave me a mean look and walked away.

I wished I could remember my name, but I supposed if I did Daddy would only be angrier. I wouldn't try any more.

Another indication of reincarnation was my mother's behavior before the birth of her eighth child. While she was carrying Jim she talked about Dad's great uncle, who had grown up with Grandpa in the farmhouse next door. Young James Pace had worked in the lumber camps of northern Michigan. In 1888 he drowned while transporting logs on St. Mary's River.

All the while she was expecting little Jim, Mom talked about Uncle James, whom she had only known through Grandpa. Although they had rarely mentioned him before the pregnancy, my parents named their youngest child after a man who had lived years before them. When Jimmy was three months old we moved into the house where his great uncle had been born ninety-nine years before.

My baby brother was smart, but he got into a lot of trouble. When he was two he tore a slat from his crib and went to the bathroom in the middle of the night. Dad had to remove part of the ladder of the windmill when four-year-old Jimmy tried to climb to the top. Nothing was safe from the child. He broke the toaster, the iron, and many toys. One day Mom missed her wooden spoons; that night she found them under Jimmy's pillow.

Just before he graduated from high school, Jim signed up with the navy. Once he nearly fell off a ship. Not long after that he narrowly escaped a collision while riding his motorcycle. On leave he demolished a new car when he hit a telephone pole, but Jim climbed out of the wreck with only a scratch on his nose.

I don't know whether great-uncle James' fall into the river was the last of many accidents, but clumsiness and impulsivity seem to run in our family. Maybe that was why I wasn't allowed to drive my parents' car. When I was young it was our only good vehicle, too precious to risk. Paradoxically, my parents' caution worked in my favor. I never told anyone, but I was glad no one encouraged me to drive. The fear of crashing into something, maybe killing somebody, has always been with me. I didn't get my driver's license until the age of twenty-six, and thoughts of a collision still torment me, although I have never been in a serious accident of any kind. The hypnotic regressions led me to believe the feeling, like my long-standing fears of ulcers and birds, is left over from another lifetime.

Reincarnation is not accepted in the Catholic religion, the faith of my parents, grandparents, and those who came before them. However, I knew from the beginning Catholicism was not for me. I was never comfortable in church--I didn't belong. Many Saturday nights I cried when trying to memorize catechism lessons I didn't understand, and Sunday mass bored me.

I learned little in religious instruction classes. In first grade we were asked to memorize junior-high level material, with words such as extreme unction, the sacrament of the dead. There were so many rules to learn, so many sins, that I became discouraged.

The nun who taught us was known as the meanest in the school, and I hated to go to class. The children were terrified as she strutted between the aisles in her black and white habit, swinging her rosary. We were all sinners, and sinners should have millstones tied around their necks and be thrown into the river. There was a large river nearby, and sometimes I imagined her throwing us into it, which chilled me. I wanted to stay home Sunday mornings, where it was safe.

Sister Charles had little respect for protestant religions. She would point to the small white church on the next street and remark, "That church was made by man. Only the Catholic church was started by God." This didn't seem fair as I attended a public school with children who went to that church, and they were good to me. Of course I was too afraid of Sister Charles to defend them.

The next year, when the time for first communion arrived, I tried to get out of it because I would be going against something inside of me. I couldn't accept what the church said Catholics must believe, and it would be wrong.

My parents insisted I "make" my first communion, and there was little a seven-year-old could do. Mom bought me a dress I didn't want and sewed a veil with a headpiece she had copied from the one she had worn as a bride. All the other girls had bought veils from the church, and I felt embarrassed. But at least I had a purse and prayer book like the other girls.

The prayer book was the only part of the first communion outfit I liked. It was shiny white with a pretty picture of the child Jesus on the cover. The edges of the pages were gold, and inside the front cover was a small crucifix.

I held up the girls' line when it came time to receive communion. "I can't swallow the host," I whispered to the priest. After his encouragement failed he asked me to move on. I returned to the pew defeated, the host stuck to the roof of my mouth. In a few moments I peeled it off with my tongue and swallowed it. I felt empty and confused, and I wanted to hide.

As I grew I continued to drift away from the church. It seemed senseless that a soul would suffer eternal damnation for eating meat on Friday or missing mass on Sunday.

In high school the church's views on sex made me angry. It was as if sex were a dirty thing, to be done only when necessary, for reproduction. Masturbation, French kissing, petting, and going steady when a couple was not able to marry in a year were all sins. Any birth control but the rhythm method was a sin. It was a sin to even think about sex. I disagreed with the church; sex could be a wonderful expression of love.

I had my own beliefs on other matters as well, and I cherished my right to think and to make up my own mind. This was not in harmony with the teachings of the authoritarian church. It seemed to operate by attempting to frighten its members into submission rather than trying to win their loyalty through love.

I was about to give up on the church when I had a mystical experience on my sixteenth birthday. It was on a Sunday, and with pride I put on my favorite dress, a two-piece green check with a ruffle at the edge of the sleeve and lace on the full skirt. I wore the whimsy my mother had made with coarse veiling and a big green flower. Dad took my brother, sisters and me to church. Before the service we knelt to pray, and as a high mass was scheduled the church was packed.

I looked at the altar, and goose pimples appeared on my arms, for I saw something I had never expected to see in church. Flying over the statues of Jesus, Mary, and Joseph was a bat, and I **knew** it had come for me. Afraid it would catch itself in my whimsy, I crouched on the kneeler, trying to hide from it. The bat flew over the heads of the people in front of me. Then it was almost upon me, and I was terrified. As I knelt it landed behind me, in my seat. Trapped between my family and another I could not escape.

I whimpered and squeezed toward the other family. Dad struck the bat with his prayer book, stilling it. In a moment an usher came and whisked it away in the collection basket, like an offering.

I shook inside for several minutes, until the visiting priest appeared in a processional with a group of altar boys. As was customary with a high mass, he sauntered up the aisle spreading incense. My eyes were on him as he approached the altar, and an amazing thing happened--I saw a pure white aura about his head. It lasted only a few seconds, but it was so beautiful I will remember it the rest of my life.

This was the only time I have ever seen an aura. Why did I experience it then? It might have been because of my relationship with Father Timothy. He had conducted a retreat the week before, which I had attended. In confession I discussed my problems with the faith, and he compared me with the infertile soil the word of God had fallen upon. To keep my faith I would have to make a special effort, attending church daily and praying frequently. I didn't think this would help, but he could offer nothing more.

Father was preoccupied with his own needs, even inside the confessional. When I sought absolution for impure thoughts he seemed to think I was guilty of more serious sins. I told him I avoided boys, but he asked me if I had feelings for him. He discussed sex in a way Father McNeill, our parish priest, never explained it, and I felt my face flush. I left the confessional filled with guilt and shame.

For weeks I struggled to understand the meaning of the aura. At last I decided to forgive Father; he was probably struggling with celibacy, and I thought priests should be allowed to marry. But was there a broader meaning to my seeing the aura? If, like Father Timothy, the church were imperfect maybe I should give it another chance.

I remained with the church until my junior year in college. It had taught me to respect others, and I appreciated its schools and aid to the needy, but I couldn't accept Catholic doctrine. Upon leaving I declared myself an agnostic, which made me feel vulnerable. What would happen when I died? I feared it would be the end of my existence. Sometimes I prayed for religious faith, although I wasn't sure anyone was listening. Full of anxiety and doubt, I drifted until hypnotic regressions and research into past lives convinced me life continued after death.

Chapter Two

Transformation

After I received my degrees in psychology and was teaching at a Detroit college I married Nat, a former mathematics teacher. Originally from Minnesota, he had come to the Detroit area to work for Chrysler, but he was laid off in the recession of 1975, less than a year after we were married. We moved south when he accepted a job at a textile company.

In the south I experienced a change in consciousness--my mind opened to the psychic world. I went with a traditional view of life; I was a realist who had little interest in e.s.p. and related phenomena. The paranormal didn't seem important to me, so I never assigned textbook chapters on altered states to my psychology students.

The change started just before my thirtieth birthday, when I began to crave music from the 1930's and `40's. On a trip to Atlanta I bought Big Band records and played them again and again. In December of 1975 I had an unusual dream. An alien on a spacecraft read a list of names. When the being came to mine the vehicle swerved and landed. The entities inside looked at me and my human companions, then assumed very slender forms, with pointed feet. Explaining they needed me, the beings took me into their craft. The queen stared at my hand and arm and decided not to take me to their planet, but I was to visit their space station on Earth for analysis.

Frightened, I remained on the ship, and the queen tried to destroy me. She lured me into a closet-like box and blew it up with a small atomic weapon. By some miracle I survived. When the queen left the scene I ran to the most remote part of the ship and hid. Slightly injured, I was discovered by the leader. I told him of the queen's treachery, and he promised to turn her into a snake.

He chanted, and she went limp. Then he gave her an injection, which froze her. The leader named me the new queen, and I became his mistress.

We married, and two children were born on the ship. When we arrived on the home planet the king welcomed us. Families were rare.

With the dream and other occurrences, I acknowledged changes in myself and sought new experiences. I normally had little interest in movie stars, but the summer I was thirty a book on Doris Day appealed to me. It discussed her love for animals and mentioned a dog named Strongheart, who had extraordinary abilities. I read about him and concluded animals have e.s.p., but most people don't recognize this ability in them, or in themselves.

In the library I found COSMIC CONSCIOUSNESS, (1) which opened my mind. In his book Richard Bucke described characteristics of the enlightened, who went through sudden, unexpected experiences which changed their views of life and death. After enlightenment they knew they were immortal and lost their fear of death.

Most of those experiencing cosmic consciousness were between thirty and forty, and their illumination came in the spring or early summer. The majority rejected wealth, convenience, and impressing others. They had great ideas and achieved their goals, often amazing the people they knew. Although they were confused after illumination, they later mellowed, finding inner peace and happiness in time.

When I read COSMIC CONSCIOUSNESS I was unhappy. I missed family and friends in Michigan and wished to escape. In March of 1977, a few weeks after I had read the book, Mohari came to me in my sleep, changing my life forever.

In the dream it seemed as if I were two entities, one a woman on a spaceship, the other a spirit watching a man make love to her. The room was small and colorless; the only furniture was a marble-like slab. Partially clothed, both the man and woman were slender, and the man was tall. The spirit near the ceiling felt the woman's pleasure. When my husband accidentally awakened me I scolded him for taking me away from a world of peace, love, and perfect happiness.

Feeling compelled to record my experience, I got out of bed. At 3:30 a.m. I went to my desk and began writing, not of the dream itself, but of the people, and the world in which they lived. They were humanoid and lived on a planet outside our galaxy. For eons they had watched life develop on Earth, guiding man's evolution. Mohari was the humanoid in the spaceship. He and Anna, the Earthwoman in the dream, were lovers.

That morning Mohari took hold of my mind, haunting me for more than a year, and I wondered if I were going crazy. During that time I felt forced to write notes about him and his planet. This was not the normal motivation which drives people to work, to complete a task. At times I felt as if a force were bearing down upon me from above, nearly crushing me mentally. Mohari seemed so real I thought I would find him sitting in my living room. He would be about thirty-five, tall and slender, with wise brown eyes. He would want to take me away, into the unknown. Frightened and confused, I didn't want to go.

What was happening to me? My knowledge of psychology was of little help. A therapist might consider me mentally ill, but I was not, at least in the usual sense. I didn't see, hear, taste, touch, or smell anything unusual. Strong convictions about the alien and his world were absent. I was unsure my writing had any basis in reality. Despite the pressure on my head I didn't feel any physical distortion, as many psychotics do.

Later the mystery began to unravel when I read THE DREAM MAKERS.(2) A dream such as that of Mohari and Anna involves a tear between the conscious and unconscious; it is like a peak experience, giving the dreamer new awareness. It forces the dreamer to face a hidden part of the self, and sometimes it refuses to release him. I was relieved to learn I was not alone in my ordeal.

In the same year (1977) Gail Sheehy wrote in PASSAGES (3) people feel a new vitality around age thirty. During their

13

twenties they neglect the inner part of themselves while working on their careers and relationships, and as they approach thirty that overlooked aspect screams for attention.

Carl Jung (4) would have agreed. He thought disregarded issues came to the attention of those at the beginning of middle age. When one of his patients was troubled by dreams of an ape, Jung said the scientist's instinctive personality was coming through. The dreamer had developed his intellectual side to the neglect of his instincts, and he had lost his balance.

Perhaps my mind was telling me it was time to pay attention to my emotional needs, to give them an outlet by working on my science fiction novel. I had been writing since childhood and had started the novel shortly after my marriage. My creative writing teacher in Michigan had praised the beginning. It had been put aside when we moved, and I hadn't realized how much writing enriched my life until I began jotting notes on Mohari's world. To get back into writing I joined a science fiction writers' group. Members read and discussed their stories and poems, and they published the best in a yearly anthology. I didn't submit anything for publication.

I hesitated to write because I no longer read science fiction. I loved Jules Verne and H.G. Wells, but modern science fiction, with its gadgetry and lack of characterization, didn't appeal to me. Fantasy was more to my taste. A friend had recommended the books of Ursula LeGuin, and I had begun reading and enjoying her tales of magic, but I wasn't writing, and I missed it.

When I met Marlene I got a different perspective on my dream. My student in an introductory psychology class at the university, Marlene was a mother who had decided to get her degree before her teen-aged daughters entered college. She was also an astrologer.

Marlene often stayed after class to talk, and we became friends. She knew a man who did hypnotic regressions into past lives and asked if I were interested. The prospect sounded strange to me; I didn't believe in past lives. Ventures into the occult were for people on the edge of society, like California hippies. But I was curious, so l considered a regression.

For a week I thought about it. There was the dream and Mohari's haunting. Could this be related to a past life? If I didn't accept Marlene's offer I might never have another chance to find out. After school was out in the spring of 1978, I made an appointment with Mark Taylor.

The hypnotist's home was in the mountains, over an hour's drive from us. Since I hadn't met the man, and the area was unfamiliar to me, I asked my husband to come with me. As we made our way in the mountains we sang "We're off to see the wizard".

The house was a sprawling ranch in a wooded area, on the bank of a small river. Mr. Taylor, an inventor and manufacturer of such products as a contact lens cleaner, worked with his engineering staff by day, and he did hypnotic regressions during his free time, often in the evenings. He was tall, slender, and reserved, with an air of sadness about him. I thought the bearded man looked like one of El Greco's religious figures.

We drank and munched on cookies in the living room, which overlooked the river. "I've never been hypnotized," I told Mr. Taylor. "I have a strong will, and I don't know if I can go under."

"That's not important," he replied. "In my twenty years of experience I've found it's imagination that counts.

"Oh, I have a great imagination," I said, feeling uneasy. A person with a good imagination could create past lives. But I was there to understand my dream, not spin a wild past life story. I would work with Mr. Taylor.

Lying on the comfortable sofa I went into a trance with ease. Mr. Taylor took me far into the past, and I recalled a life as an American Indian living in the woodlands. I was a young man with tanned skin and large muscles, of which I was proud. Mr. Taylor took me back further, and as a little boy I danced and beat a drum trimmed with feathers. Life was good, and I was filled with joy.

At the end of the session Mr. Taylor told me I would remember everything afterward. As if awakening from a long nap, I would be refreshed. After reorienting myself I did feel renewed, but what I had said surprised me. I left the house stunned, confused. Thinking I knew myself and what my life was about, I had been confident, but the realization I might have been someone else long ago threw me off balance.

As we drove home that humid night in late spring, I felt uneasy because of the many curves in the two-lane mountain road, curves that were not easy to follow in the darkness. And there were big trucks traveling in the opposite direction. Too late we saw a rabbit crossing our path. Bump. We hit it. Poor bunny. The rabbit's death made me feel even more uncomfortable as we drove home.

The next time I saw Mr. Taylor was in late August. I had spent most of the summer in Michigan. In June I had taken my usual vacation, and in early August my father had died. During that time Mr. Taylor had moved into a new home, which was still under construction. Marlene and I visited the large contemporary structure in the woods, and Mr. Taylor and I made plans for future regression sessions.

Before our next meeting Marlene took me to a luncheon with members of her psychic group. There I met Dr. Danfield, a college professor who did life readings, like Edgar Casey. I discussed my life as an Indian with him and asked if he would do a reading for me. He wouldn't be available for several weeks, but he promised to find time for me.

In the fall I was occupied with classes, so I had only one regression with Mr. Taylor, to the life of a peasant woman in fifteenth century Europe. I had borne six children, led a good life, and was an old woman when I died. After the funeral the townspeople celebrated my life by singing and dancing.

Marlene and I spent little time together that fall; she was busy with an accelerated French course. She did recommend THE NATURE OF PERSONAL REALITY, (5) a Seth book by Jane Roberts.

I read it, but I was not ready for concepts such as people creating physical reality through their beliefs. I bought SETH SPEAKS, (6) and it made more sense to me. It reassured me a sort of Heaven exists after death, and a person's experience depends upon the kind of life she led and what she expects. If a woman believes she has led a life worthy of an eternity in Hell, she experiences it, until other souls convince her she is wrong. Then she will be able to learn from her mistakes.

Roberts' explanation of different realms in the afterlife fascinated me. In a world of pure thought spirits can write books in an instant. After struggling with writing for years I could appreciate this.

In 1978 I also read Targ and Puthoff's book on remote viewing, MIND REACH, (7) which opened my mind to e.s.p.. I had never before heard of remote viewing, where an experimenter goes to a place chosen at random and a study participant describes the scene when no information on the "target" area is provided for him.

The experiments with Uri Geller amazed me. Strange coincidences had occurred--among them a photograph of a disembodied arm over Uri's head, taken in a study. One night after he had snapped the picture the photographer had awakened to see the apparition of an arm floating over his bed. Most amazing of all, a photocopy of MIND REACH's chapter on Geller had disintegrated in the files. The ideas in the book excited me, and I shared them with my students that semester. Then I spoke briefly about hypnotic regressions and invited them to Mr. Taylor's home for a presentation after the semester had ended.

I spent the holidays in Michigan and returned to the south in January. Before teaching my afternoon class I went to Mr. Taylor's house for regressions. As his engineering staff worked in the lower level, I recalled past lives upstairs. After I came out of hypnosis I felt refreshed, full of energy. Classes went well.

Our winter sessions focused on the dream of Mohari. By then I wasn't as driven to find a past life connection with him. Mohari had gradually released me, and after my father's death his grip was gone. The pressure on the top of my head had ceased, an indication Mohari had detached himself from me. (8) Gone also was the compulsion to write about Mohari's world. Had my father helped rid me of my obsession?

I had tried to make contact with him at the funeral home. One morning when I was alone I prayed, begging Dad to give me a sign he was present. Anything, even a flickering candle would do. I was still an agnostic, uncertain of survival after death, but I wanted to believe in immortality.

There was no sign. Maybe Dad didn't have the power to show his presence. Or perhaps there was no life after death. I wept in frustration.

Then he came to me in a surprising way, in my mind. "I'm sorry," he said one day, when I wasn't thinking of him. I didn't have to ask what he meant, for he had hurt me deeply by his rejection after my brother was born. Until then we had been close, but he hadn't needed me once he had Loren.

Maybe Mohari no longer needed me now he had revealed himself and his world. But I was still curious about a past life relationship with him. Mr. Taylor helped me explore it under hypnosis. We discovered I had been Anna, the Earthwoman in the dream. Her first name and that of her husband Jake came easily, but it took two sessions to get their last name, Randall. In the initial session I could only recall the first syllable. The last one came in the second session, with much effort.

The name of the New England city, and Marshall, the street where the Randalls lived, were easy to remember. Perhaps they had been triggered by looking at a map of the area a year before the hypnotic session. I had come upon a map of the major highways of the United States at the back of a road atlas. Marshall, a point on the coast of New England, was the only such feature labeled on the map. I wondered why. The area seemed important to me, for an unknown reason. I closed my eyes and concentrated on it, but nothing came to mind. Later, hypnosis unlocked my memory.

The following is a summary of the sessions on the life of Anna.

Anna was born in New York City, the only child of a couple killed in an auto accident. Her grandparents raised her in a small New England city. Anna quit high school to marry and soon gave birth to two children. Like her grandfather, Jake abused Anna. He was often drunk, and she suspected there were other women in his life.

In the initial regressions I spoke of the abduction of Anna and Jake by aliens as they traveled in New England. Their car seemed controlled by a space craft, and Jake slumped over the steering wheel. Anna felt compelled to open the car door. She walked into a wooded area, where humanoids led her into their ship, which took off and then was "swallowed" by a mother ship. In the second craft she detected a sinister atmosphere, and she tried to leave. Spider-like creatures, with black under their eyes and rapidly moving limbs, dragged a terrified Anna to an examination room, where she lost consciousness. Later Mohari admitted she had been inseminated as part of an experiment, but she and Jake had forgotten the entire incident.

In another regression I pictured the family on a camping trip in 1943. During their stay in the woods Anna met Mohari. Her husband had left the campground to go drinking, and Anna had put her children to bed when she glimpsed a tall, attractive man.

Mohari told her he was a visitor from far away. When Jake didn't return they went deep into the woods together, to Mohari's ship. The ship didn't frighten Anna; she entered it without hesitation. He gave her a drink which affected her like alcohol and told her she reminded him of his deceased wife, a beautiful blonde woman. Alia had died when a piece of space junk hit her as they walked on a beach of Barbon, their planet.

He had never recovered from her death many years before. Mohari felt rejected when Alia refused to inhabit the new body provided for her. Shortly afterward he signed up with a project headquartered on a space station not far from Earth.

Mohari had a special connection with Earth. An ancestor had worked there eons ago, when man was developing. Since then his people had watched over the planet. Mohari felt at home on Earth; he liked its people. But he was worried about the war.

Anna was drawn to Mohari, and the next night she went to him. They made love, and he asked her to accompany him when he left Earth. As she didn't want to leave her children, she refused.

The next day she went home with her husband and children, but she couldn't get Mohari out of her mind. Several nights later, while her drunken husband slept, she returned to the campground. Mohari was waiting in the door of the ship. In a few hours they left, heading toward a space station.

For several years they traveled in space. Anna lost a feeling for time. There were no days or nights, no weekends. Mohari, Anna, and two children born on the ship were on a four-hour-sleeping, four-hour-waking schedule.

As the time to visit the station approached Anna became excited. She was eager to meet the representatives of different planets meeting to discuss evolving life in other worlds. Mohari told her they would use telepathy to communicate, and she spent much time practicing it.

Excitement turned to apprehension as the ship approached the station. Anna felt doomed. She feared she would never again see her children on Earth. When the craft wobbled as it neared its destination, Anna screamed in terror. Seconds later the ship, out of control, crashed into the edge of the station, killing Anna, Mohari, and their children.

In luminous white sacks they floated to Earth. Just above the planet Mohari slipped away from Anna and the children, moving in a different direction. Anna felt calm, weightless, as she drifted toward Earth. Other sacks floated down with her and the children; some took a different course from theirs.

In time she became a crying baby in the arms of a mother with a brown pageboy. It was 1946.

From the time I underwent hypnosis to help me understand my dream of Mohari, I wondered about the process. What is hypnosis? Why were some able to recall past lives under its influence? After the regressions I began reading about it.

The nature of hypnosis is controversial. There is no definition psychologists and psychiatrists agree upon, but muscle relaxation, drowsiness, great suggestibility, improved imagination, recall of material from the past, and less desire for activity are involved. Hypnosis is not sleep according to psychological and physiological measures, but there is heightened concentration with little awareness of surroundings.

Hypnosis resembles sleep in that sleepers and those hypnotized experience a short period of semi-consciousness as they come out of these states. Afterward they may have headaches or feel dizzy. The headaches are caused by changes in blood vessels among other alterations. (9)

Dr. Raymond Moody discussed hypnagogic states, between normal waking and consciousness, and sleep, in COMING BACK. (10) In this twilight area the person is neither asleep nor awake. Here he observes what the unconscious provides but is aware of the surroundings. These states are linked to creativity, and Thomas Edison used them when he catnapped to solve a problem.

The essential difference between sleep and hypnosis is in the subjects' response to suggestion. When under hypnosis a person can laugh, cry, or walk around the room if it is suggested. In this state one feels drowsy and fatigued, and her eyes are tired. Then she relaxes. These same feelings are present when falling asleep or upon awakening, only in hypnosis the state is induced and prolonged.

As might be expected good sleepers are generally easier to hypnotize than poor sleepers. Other factors which affect the success of hypnosis are intelligence, a strong will, imagination, and concentration. Creative people are susceptible to hypnosis, perhaps because they engage in unregulated thinking.

Is hypnosis an altered state? This has generated a lot of controversy; there are three points of view. One state theory claims all hypnotized individuals share a set of psychological characteristics, but a phenomenon has never been found that consistently occurs in all hypnotic subjects (amnesia, for example) that is not found in a state other than hypnosis.

Another state concept is looser, with no causes or defining features given. In this view whether hypnosis is a special state of consciousness is not important, and questions such as the underlying mechanisms of hypnosis can be considered without concern for it.

Prominent psychologist E.R. Hilgard proposed an explanation for hypnosis--dissociation, or a separation of consciousness into streams of mental activity. When one or more of these streams affects experience, thought, and action outside of awareness and control, dissociation occurs, as in amnesia. This involves lack of awareness. Voluntary control is lost in automatic writing and when posthypnotic suggestions are carried out.

A third view focuses on hypnosis as social behavior. A person's internal state is not considered here. He takes on the role of a hypnotized person as the hypnotist and the culture define it. If he has the skills required for the role, and a sympathetic audience, he may perform well. A man who has studied German, for example, will likely be able to convince an audience believing in reincarnation he was a German army officer in the second world war.

It is not necessary to choose between theories of hypnosis as an internal state or as an interpersonal phenomenon as both contribute to our understanding of it. The social view interests me most as my experience supports it. The first regressions to Anna's life resembled Betty and Barney Hill's abduction by extraterrestrials. When I came out of hypnosis I was embarrassed, ashamed of what I had said. Why had I repeated a story so similar to those of many others? Had I been connecting with a reservoir of common human experience, or had I told the story to get Mr. Taylor's reaction?

Mr. Taylor had seemed open to the idea of extraterrestrial visitors, and he encouraged me to tell the complete story, but I sensed he enjoyed the romance between Anna and Mohari most of all. This might have been because of difficulty in a relationship of his own. We spent a lot of time talking about Anna and Mohari, and I might have embellished the story to please him. Nevertheless, this does not invalidate the entire experience.

Distortion in past life regressions has occurred before.

Under hypnosis Jennie Cockell, (11) who found her family from a past life, gave the names of four of her children as James, Mary, Harry and Kathy. Only two of the names were correct. Mary was the eldest daughter and Jeffrey James the second son. Their surname was Sutton, not O'Neil, as Mrs. Cockell had said while hypnotized. She had doubted its accuracy as it was "offered with unlikely clarity", (12) and Mary's husband's name, Bryan O'Neil, was too close to the familiar Ryan O'Neal.

Morey Bernstein observed Bridey Murphy's memory was sharper in some sessions than in others. At first Bridey called herself Friday, and once she made a mistake in her age at marriage. Bridey Murphy might have upgraded the status of both her father and her husband to barrister. No records could be found of the law practices of either, but there is some evidence her husband was an accountant. (13) Perhaps Bridey was an habitual braggart, but maybe Ruth Simmons thought hypnotist Morey Bernstein would be impressed by her status as the daughter, and later wife, of a barrister.

Ruth probably wasn't conscious of any deception. People can behave in unusual ways while hypnotized. A subject may experience a double hallucination, where he or she "sees" and interacts with an imaginary person in an empty chair. When the hypnotized individual is informed the real person is sitting outside his field of vision, the subject keeps the hallucination of the person in the chair. He also retains the idea of the person out of his sight, and is confused. This is called "trance logic", thought that allows two contradictory conditions to exist at the same time. Non-hypnotized subjects don't experience this, and researchers do not understand it. (14)

Another hypnotic phenomenon is the hidden observer. After an hypnotized person's pain has been relieved, for example, part of that person may still feel and be able to report the discomfort. Hilgard, who found the hidden observer while studying pain, views it as dissociation to prevent the pain from becoming conscious.

The hidden observer is present in about half of study participants, and all of them are highly suggestible. It is nearly always present in those who can see themselves as both children, and adult observers in hypnotic age regression, experiencing two different states at once. (15)

During the past-life regressions I could either look at a previous personality from above or enter that individual, sometimes with Mr. Taylor's encouragement. Dissociation was also present in the dream of Mohari and Anna, in which I was at once observing them from above and experiencing Anna's sensations and feelings.

I consider myself suggestible, and this helps make me a good hypnotic subject, able to take two points of view. Highly hypnotizable people have other characteristics in common. Many have had mystical experiences, such as traveling out of their bodies. I have seen an aura.

What enables some hypnotic subjects to recall past lives might be their openness to the paranormal, which they share with others who believe in extrasensory perception and related phenomena. Believers in psychic phenomena, who are more likely to be female than male, have been found to be religious empiricists who learn from experience and disregard theories. Those who do not believe in psychic phenomena rely on theory and reject experiences which fail to fit into their framework. Believers remember their dreams better than others and work to interpret them, (16) which I have done.

I felt exhilarated after reading these studies. Despite my unusual experiences nothing was wrong. People like me, with a mystical orientation, were simply different from the bulk of humanity. No wonder I had never been comfortable with the Catholic religion and its dogma, for the beliefs were abstract, like theories, and I operated according to my experiences.

I began to see my style as a strength. It enabled me to know myself, and by relying on my feelings and perceptions I could better understand others, and the world. In paying attention to my experiences rather than the thoughts of others I was free to soar into the unknown without restraint, and I loved it.

Chapter Three

Obsession and Reincarnation

During the regressions I felt close to Mohari, and wished to be with him. On Valentine's Day of 1979 I went into a deep hypnotic trance and recalled his life with Anna. The next morning I awoke in tears, longing to join Mohari. I had never loved anyone so intensely. This was madness, but I didn't care. If he had come for me then I would have gone, oblivious to what the future held. Let him sweep me away onto his craft and into the unknown. I would leave this world if only I could be with him.

The obsession continued for more than a week. My husband was a stranger, and I resented his intrusion on my fantasy. I wanted to escape life, to be alone with my thoughts. I dragged myself through the day, managing to do the essentials: teaching classes, shopping, straightening the house. Between my tasks I retreated into a fog, where tears filled my eyes. I wished the sadness would go away, but I couldn't garner the strength to help myself.

In desperation I resumed work on the science fiction novel shelved nearly five years before. Maybe Mohari would let me go if I completed the story about his ancestor. But writing didn't change my mood. Then the breakthrough came, and I began to recover. Days after the Valentine's Day session I awoke with a realization. Because Anna had died with Mohari in the crash, she hadn't been able to mourn him. More than thirty years later I was grieving, putting our relationship to rest. But it was disturbing my life. I had to regain control.

Years later, after reading GODDESSES IN EVERYWOMAN, (1) I reflected on what had happened. Bolen speaks of the sacred marriage. When it comes in a dream the experience is awesome and symbolic of the "intrapsychic union between masculine and feminine". The sacred marriage represents wholeness.

Experiencing Anna and Mohari's union moved me greatly, as similar dreams did for those in Bolen's book. It seemed more real than ordinary life, and there was the feeling of a deep joy and peace I had never before experienced. I count it among the most important events of my life.

For years I had searched for a soul mate, a man with whom I could share my inner self. He would be a lot like me, with the same values, a similar outlook on life. I had known a lot of men in college, gone on blind dates arranged by friends, and joined a computer dating service, but a soul mate eluded me.

At the age of twenty-six I had a serious talk with myself. "Look, Marie," I said. "It's getting late. Maybe your standards are too high. There are decent men out there. Sure their backgrounds are different from yours. Granted some are overweight or balding." I looked into the mirror. "But you're not perfect either. You've got to take a chance before it's too late."

With that I joined the second computer dating club to find a husband. I received five names for a small fee; one of them was Nat's. I was immediately attracted to his dark good looks and impressed with his knowledge of history and science. He was shy, and sometimes he stuttered on our first dates, but I found it endearing. He was a sweet guy. The next year we were married.

Despite our layoffs and move to the south, where I was homesick, I had faith in our marriage. Then came the dream of Mohari and perfect love. He was the soul mate I had longed for, but he lived only in my mind. I needed to see him, talk with him, touch him. Frustrated, I alternately wished to be with him and hoped he would leave me alone. Had he come into my life to torment me? Seeking an answer I continued with the regressions.

In the next session I gave Anna's address. The street name resembled that of the point I had seen on the U.S. map in the road atlas. I also discovered Anna and Jake had had a third child. As an infant Jake had died of pneumonia.

My longest regression occurred two weeks later, when I summarized Anna's life. The session went smoothly. I gave a detailed, cohesive account of her life, which included such information as her maiden name, Garfield. Mr. Taylor invited me to stay for dinner, and we talked about our plans for the future. I would move back to Michigan, where I would research and write a book on Anna's life. He hoped to make his first million soon. Then he would retire from manufacturing to do hypnotic research full time.

After the regressions I felt a new appreciation for Earth. I was glad to be here, but continued to gaze into the starry sky and wonder what lay beyond, as I had since childhood.

The heavens had always fascinated me, and I started reading science fiction at an early age. In third grade my favorite book was THE WONDERFUL FLIGHT TO THE MUSHROOM PLANET. (2) I wanted to become an astronomer and discover new worlds, until I learned advanced math was required, not my strength.

At the time of the last regressions my mind was filled with more practical concerns than life on other planets. Nat and I had never been comfortable in the south, and we missed friends and family. It seemed we had fulfilled our purpose in the region, with Nat learning about textiles and my teaching and regression experiences. My husband had been searching for a job in the north for months, and at last a desirable Michigan company showed interest.

Reading the Seth books and talking to Marlene had taught me I could have anything if I imagined it. Visualization is a powerful tool, and I used it, seeing Nat and myself back in Michigan over the months of the job search.

In March of 1979 Nat accepted a job with the Michigan firm. He would work on an electric car, and on batteries which would store electricity at power plants for peak consumption hours.

I responded to the news by singing and waltzing around the house. My only regret was leaving Marlene, Mr. Taylor, and the neighbors, who had been good to us. Marlene was sorry to lose me, but she understood my need to go home. Before I left she made an appointment for me with Dr. Danfield. On a March afternoon I drove to the nearby town where Peter Danfield lived. He did life readings in the living room of his modest home, where his wife guided him. Dr. Danfield went into a trance and contacted two of my spirit guides, Loyolia, a beautiful blonde, and Bertram, a stern, red-faced man I recognized as my father.

They warned me through Dr. Danfield: "Do not overdo spiritual awareness; it can harm you mentally, emotionally, physically, and spiritually." They also encouraged me: "You have a positive mental attitude, and that is good. You can get whatever you desire, providing you do not hurt anyone. You have good awareness and are arising to higher spiritual awareness planes. You have been given the ability to retain the dream state."

"What does that mean?" I asked.

"It means you will remember important dreams," replied Dr. Danfield. "Messages come through the sleep state. When you are asleep you work with people who need your assistance. When you awake not feeling rested you have been busy. When you awaken with a jolt it is because of the shock of returning to your body."

"But I feel a jolt if something disturbs one of my daydreams," I said.

"You must want to leave your body."

I asked about my Indian life, as Mr. Taylor and I had spent little time on it. Dr. Danfield said I had been White Cloud, a young Indian living near Lake Erie. He was a peacemaker, respected by both Indians and Whites, but some young men envied him and arranged his death.

"When he was setting his traps to catch animals they captured him, tied him, and took him to a high rock ledge. The punishment was to spread him on his back and tie him down and allow the big birds to come in and destroy the physical form. These were the ones known as eagles. . . He kept them off as long as he could by noise with (his) mouth but soon became so weak he could not, and then the birds ripped him apart--the large eagle bird(s). They (the young men) put the body close to a nesting area and of course this made them (the eagles) come in more fierce than ever before. That is the way the physical form was ended at that time."

"How old was he?" asked Mrs. Danfield.

After some hesitation her husband answered. "He was nineteen when he died."

"Did he have a mate?" she asked.

"He had not taken a mate. A white-skinned lady liked him very much, but he did not have much to do with others. He wanted to trap and hunt his own way. He learned ways to prevent illness in himself. He went to a high place and looked to the skies and especially the sun and breathed in health from the sun. He breathed in health from the big light in the sky at night-- the moon. He learned to control the inner self well."

"What happened to the boys who killed him?" Mrs. Danfield wanted to know.

"Two braves caused his death. They were caught by two white men who liked White Cloud. They (the white men) did something similar to the braves, but they did not know how to make the birds come. Animals came and destroyed the braves (who were tied up).

At last I had a satisfying explanation for my fear of birds. My early fear of driving a car was another puzzle. I asked Dr. Danfield why I had been afraid to drive.

"There is a bubble . . . a sphere. It is not a helicopter.

I have not seen . . . A kind of silver dome apparatus. They appear to be partly human. They are from another planet, more highly developed mentally and spiritually than those on the Earth plane." He hesitated. "I cannot get a place. It looks sandy, but . . ."

"She is a well-developed person. The hair appears to be reddish brown."

"The entities seem to have shiny material over normal clothing. They are lifting off. She reaches to hit another button, but someone stops the hand. We aren't allowed to rise much further. There seems to be oxygen enough. They have gone up and moved out over the water."

"There is a hole in the water, as though a vortex. They are going down into it. They will not let me enter. There is an island . . . We are up observing this, above looking down. That must be Bermuda, Bermuda Island."

"Is this Marie?" Mrs. Danfield interrupted.

"It appears to be. Yes. We are hovering over to see if there is some way to enter."

At this point Dr. Danfield reported a voice from the (Akashic) Record. (3) "It is not yet for you to see. You will be allowed at another time to enter and describe what is in this area," it said.

He continued, "Pain over the right eye, as if the head has struck something. It does damage to the eye. It is the pressure. Locked with someone. Problem of bends going into the water."

He changed his focus. "Parting of ways with the husband. She was assisting the needy, and he was discouraged about not having more time with her. He decided to go his way. Both were released. She was taken below the surface in a domed vehicle."

"Any children?" Mrs. Danfield asked.

"None at that time."

"How old was she?"

"Twenty-four when taken."

"What was the purpose?"

"To learn the lives of others who lived in this area."

"Can we get any more information?"

"When not separated from the physical form we are not allowed certain information."

I was disappointed Dr. Danfield couldn't give more details on this life. Why I feared driving was still unclear. Later in the evening I felt remorse for White Cloud because the young man had died a horrible death. He was a peaceful person who didn't deserve it.

After Dr. Danfield's life reading I was more skeptical of hypnosis than ever. Had our discussion of White Cloud's death at a previous luncheon triggered his recall of the Indian, or had it provided the foundation for a fantasy? I regretted mentioning White Cloud to Dr. Danfield. I would forever wonder how it had affected the reading.

The Bermuda Triangle part of the session disturbed me most of all. As were my first regressions to the life of Anna, it was too trite. I doubted a life under the sea near Bermuda and concluded information obtained under hypnosis had to be carefully evaluated.

Dr. Ian Stevenson, the world-renowned researcher in reincarnation, agrees. With regard to past lives, he has found little of value in psychic readings or in hypnotic regressions.

Stevenson, a psychiatrist at the University of Virginia medical school, believes psychic readings of previous lives provide the weakest evidence for past lives. Little verifiable information has been obtained through the use of drugs, meditation, or hypnotic regressions. The best evidence comes from children's recollections of their previous lives, which are initially spontaneous.

Stevenson has concluded hypnotically induced personalities are a mixture of the current personality, the person's judgement of what the hypnotist wants, fantasies of the previous life, and perhaps information from paranormal channels.

In a few cases Dr. Stevenson feels valid information on past lives comes through hypnosis, as in Bridey Murphy and cases he has investigated in which hypnotized individuals spoke foreign languages they had not learned normally. He suggests the hypnotized individual, with his enhanced powers of concentration, may be able to dislodge memories of previous lives. In some cases fragments of a previous life might have been recalled before hypnosis.

This was true for me, as I remembered my death in a hospital before I could talk, as well as the length of my previous surname. During hypnosis I was able to give the names of Anna and Jacob, as well as their New England city.

Although Stevenson has found few verifiable details in dreams thought to be from past lives, he admits some dreams contain accurate memories. In rare cases extrasensory perception may be involved.

In FROM ASHES TO HEALING (4) many of Gershom's Holocaust victims recall dreams and visions from their past lives in World War II. A 29-year-old farmer from Nova Scotia had a series of vivid dreams from the life of a Jew in Holland. During the war he and his family hid in the root cellar of their house. It was cold and dark, but a good place to hide. A softly chiming clock occupied a table in their shelter. On the third night of his dream the farmer was told the clock sat in an antique shop near his present home. When he followed the dream's directions to the store he was shocked to find the clock.

As illustrated in the case above, scenes in dreams of supposed previous lives are realistic and coherent. "The details of the surroundings are as vivid and as natural as waking perceptions are, and they lack the bizarreness that objects and surroundings so often have in ordinary dreams." (5) These dreams stay with the person regardless of whether they are repeated; they are fixed in his memory. Stevenson has heard many such dreams, and some fit in with the dreamer's personality, expressing uncommon fears or interests in certain countries.

My dream of Anna and Mohari was vivid and coherent, and it seemed natural. It has remained with me always, and it has changed my life. As I enjoy stories of other worlds the space ship setting reflects my personality. I will probably never be able to verify this dream, but it doesn't matter to me.

The December 1975 precursor dream was extraordinary but less compelling. Both dreams involved romance on a space ship, where two children were born to an Earthwoman and a humanoid. However, in the first dream the woman survived the explosion of a nuclear device. The humanoid queen responsible for the detonation was to be transformed into a snake, which of course is unrealistic. The memory of this dream faded quickly. I was surprized to find an account in my notes.

The dream of Mohari and Anna remained in my memory, and Mohari haunted me and dominated the hypnotic regressions.

When I later read psychologist Edith Fiore's work on entity attachment the "haunting" began to make sense. (6) One of her patients affected by a troublesome entity had experienced pressure. It seemed like a heavy blanket on him which lifted after Dr. Fiore persuaded a spirit to leave him. I felt pressure on my head for weeks after my dream of Mohari, and I wondered if he had been attached to my aura, as Dr. Fiore suggested in her patient's case. When Mohari came to me in the dream I hadn't wanted to let go of him or his world, and I might have trapped him in my aura, holding him prisoner. In her book Dr. Fiore focused on spirits who chose to enter humans, but I believe a strong person can attract and keep an entity, perhaps against its will.

I have paid dearly for my "sin". At times I thought I would lose my mind. Dr. Stevenson believes the paranormal can come through in dreams and hypnosis, and the guides in Dr. Danfield's reading warned me against overzealousness in psychic exploration. I believe a part of me went overboard, and I suffered.

Fortunately it seemed Mohari didn't want to possess me; he was probably a messenger sent to help change the direction of my life. In that he was successful, and I eventually let go of him.

Coping with past-life influences is not easy, as shown in the case of Betty Riley. (7) She dreamed of a life in 17th century London, was hypnotically regressed to it, and had flashbacks.

One night, after she had viewed a mural of London created in 1666, she saw the picture when she closed her eyes to sleep. Turning on a light, she found herself in the London apartment she had seen in previous dreams, complete with large windows of multicolored small squares, a wooden fireplace, and flickering candles. Frightened, she began sobbing. The cat licking Mrs. Riley's toes brought her out of the state, and she mentally returned to her own apartment.

But the altered states continued. During the day she saw carriages and horses on dirt roads instead of cars on the expressway. Her office would disappear, and she would find herself in a theater, park, or courtyard.

Mrs. Riley sank into depression. Lacking the strength to do the simplest things, such as fix her hair or prepare a meal, she withdrew from life. She couldn't tolerate the radio or television, and she unplugged the telephone. Sometimes she had migraine headaches which lasted for three days.

The psychologist who had hypnotized Mrs. Riley refused to continue while she was depressed. He was afraid if he took her back to seventeenth century England she might prefer living there and never return to the present. She was losing touch with reality.

After a long struggle Mrs. Riley acknowledged her fears and began to deal with her emotions. She slept soundly, and the flashbacks became less vivid, more like pictures than reliving scenes from the seventeenth century. When she started writing A VEIL TOO THIN: REINCARNATION OUT OF CONTROL, (8) the flashbacks ceased.

As this case and many others illustrate, psychic development must be undertaken with care, or the result may be tragic, with mental illness or suicide as possible outcomes.

Keeping this in mind, exploring past lives, extrasensory perception, and phenomena of the spirit world, can enrich one's life. Although Mohari seemed to control me at times, leading to confusion and pain, I learned a great deal from him, and I wouldn't trade the experience. I feel he was destined to be a part of my life, pushing me in the direction of self-fulfillment when I was stagnating. Because of his appearance in my dream my thinking changed, I underwent hypnotic regressions into past lives, and read about psychic phenomena and reincarnation.

I didn't believe in reincarnation when the regressions started, but as the months wore on it "grew" on me. It was not until I returned to Michigan and read Dr. Stevenson's research that I began to understand the nature of reincarnation.

I wondered exactly what inhabited a new body. Dr. Stevenson brought forth two basic viewpoints. To a Hindu the same personality exists from one lifetime to another, but circumstances in each life change it. To a Buddhist an old personality gives rise to a new one as a low-burning candle lights another to perpetuate life. This can be called rebirth.

Dr. Stevenson has studied cases suggesting reincarnation for many years. As of 1994 he had published 68 detailed case reports and was working on more. (9)   The most compelling stories occur in areas where western culture is not dominant, such as Asia and west Africa. In western cultures, where belief in reincarnation is uncommon, a child's recollection of a past life is likely to be suppressed. Dr. Stevenson's cases from the United States are typically reported by mothers with little education beyond high school, most of them living in small towns. If they are Christians, doctrine is less important to them than Christ's teachings.

In a fully developed reincarnation case, a person predicts his rebirth before he dies, perhaps indicating whom he wishes his parents will be or where he will return. Then he dies and someone dreams he will return to that person's family. Soon a baby is born with birthmarks or defects like the wounds or markings of the deceased. When the child is old enough to speak he talks about the life of the deceased, and others observe behavior reminiscent of the dead person's.

A good example, although not a completely developed case, is that of Susan Eastland. (10) After six-year-old Winnie's death in an auto accident her sister dreamed Winnie was returning to the family. Her mother became pregnant two years later and dreamed Winnie was coming back to them. In the delivery room the baby's father thought he heard Winnie saying: "Daddy, I'm coming home."

The baby was named Susan, and when she was two she claimed she was six. She identified two of Winnie's photographs as her own. Both Susan and Winnie were aggressive and well-coordinated. They each had heavy hair growth on their backs. Susan had a small birthmark on her left hip, corresponding to the most serious external injury Winnie had received in the automobile accident which killed her.

Some children speak of their past lives before they can communicate well about the images from them. Most information involves the people and happenings of their former lives. Often their memories concern the last year, month, or days of their past lives. Three-quarters recall how the person died, and they are more likely to remember details of the death when it was violent. The time interval between death and rebirth is usually under three years.

I remember only Amanda's death scene, at the Catholic hospital with her daughter attending her. She gasped for air, stopped breathing, felt hot and trapped in her body, and thought, "I suppose this is it."

I was born three months after Amanda's death, and the images of her death scene, as well as her feelings, have been present in my mind as long as I can remember. I do not feel her personality passed into my body intact; I have always thought I have my own identity. Dr. Stevenson's (11) research is in harmony with my conclusion. He found most people recalling past lives see their own lives as distinct from the others. This favors the Buddhist interpretation of reincarnation.

As in my case, children generally remember past lives while they are awake, but sometimes scenes from another life come in dreams. Jenny Cockell (12) recalled her past-life as an Irish mother both in dreams and while awake. The dreams of Mary's dying were filled with fear for the children she was leaving. Jenny awakened in tears, and she felt Mary's guilt. However, Jenny's daytime thoughts of the children were often pleasant. Adults may encounter evidence of previous lives through past-life readings by a psychic, by hypnotic regressions, drugs, meditation, or by analyzing d'eja`-vu experiences. Dr. Stevenson has found little verifiable information in cases where these methods have been used.

Nevertheless, many people feel either they, or someone they are close to, has been reincarnated. When I discuss my hypnotic regressions people open up, sharing their experiences. Once a Tupperware supervisor claimed her husband knew he was a priest in a past life. At a Trivial Pursuit party I met a man whose father is a retired army officer and believes he was a Roman soldier. A well-known romance writer confided at a writers' gathering she remembers being choked to death in a past life.

These people acknowledge the possibility of reincarnation as an explanation for these memories. Dr. Stevenson has explored other alternatives in addition to this. They include fraud, cryptomnesia, genetic memory, e.s.p. and personation, and the survival of death, which includes possession as well as rebirth. (13)

Perhaps the most obvious possibility is fraud, but Dr. Stevenson doesn't consider it a plausible explanation for his more detailed cases. There are too many witnesses for coaching, and the gain brought about by a hoax would not be enough to encourage it. In most cases the socio-economic differences between the families of present and past incarnations are slight. The majority of past lives are obscure, and some would bring shame to present individuals. In one of the cases Dr. Stevenson investigated, a man in a past life had been a murderer.

There are risks involved in fraud. If stories of previous lives are made up, the privacy of families can be invaded. The child might run away to his alleged former family, as some children who recall past lives have done. In some cultures children are discouraged from discussing past lives as it is felt their recall dooms them to an early death.

Dr. Stevenson feels cryptomnesia, whereby a person might have learned information from a book, radio or t.v. program, or a stranger, then forgotten how he obtained it and claimed it as a past life, is an unlikely explanation for his stronger cases. Nor does Dr. Stevenson believe the amount of intimate information the child reveals about his former family could have been obtained from the limited contact the current and former families have had in the present life.

As far as non-familial influences are concerned, many of the children recalling past-lives cannot read, and radio and television are uncommon in the third world, where most of these children live. Parents in these areas tend to be protective of their children where strangers are concerned.

Regarding paranormal, or unsubstantiated causes, Dr. Stevenson considers genetic "memory" a possibility in cases of a child recalling a past life of a direct ancestor. The experiences of that life would be recorded in the child's genes. This would apply to only a small number of cases.

Extrasensory perception plus personation might help explain more cases. Here a person receives information about a previous personality through e.s.p., integrates it into his own personality, and believes he is that person. However, this does not reveal why a child in a family unknown to the previous personality would be chosen, or why the child would emulate the behavior of the deceased even if she received extrasensory images. E.s.p. alone cannot explain the incorporation into the child's personality.

In addition, the amount of information some children have on their past lives would not be known to one person. There would have to be many agents sending extrasensory messages to explain this, and such a "conspiracy" is unlikely. E.s.p. cannot account for the exhibition of skills not acquired in the current life, such as Ruth Simmons dancing the Irish morning jig. (14) Most important, extrasensory perception is a poor explanation for the years of identification with the former personality the children in Dr. Stevenson's studies exhibit. He found the motivation for this present neither in the children he interviewed, nor in most of their parents. Even if the parents encouraged such identification it would be unlikely their children could achieve it. Dr. Stevenson noted the average age of the children when they first spoke or behaved like the person in the previous life was 2.6 years. (15)

Finally, Dr. Stevenson has found no evidence of e.s.p. ability in most of the children he studied, unless the recall of past lives is considered an illustration of the phenomenon.

This leaves survival of death, by possession or rebirth, as an explanation for the recall of past lives. Possession might explain some past life recollections, but it does not generally fit children's experiences. When a person is possessed he or she retains some control of the body; the possessing spirit is not always present. When present it will identify itself as someone other than the possessed person. This inconsistency is not found in many cases of those recalling past lives.

Possession does not account for the revival of memories when the child returns to his home in a former life. It also does not explain the child's patchy memory of the past life; this resembles ordinary irregularities in memory, as in the repression of painful events. Possessing entities rarely have a memory problem. Finally, there is usually a reason for possession, an entity's revenge, for example, and this is rare in cases of those who recall past lives.

I believe Dr. Stevenson's studies provide strong evidence for rebirth, as do the Bridey Murphy case, the dreams of Betty Riley, Jenny Cockell's reunion with her past-life children, and the research of psychologist Helen Wambach.

Colorado housewife Ruth Simmons, who had never traveled to Ireland, spoke in a subtle Irish brogue while hypnotically regressed to the life of Bridey Murphy. Some of the information she gave is not available in books or through other sources in the United States. An example is her reference to Bailings Crossing, which was too small to be placed on a map. Yet two people familiar with that part of Northern Ireland verified it. Bridey also revealed some facts even the Irish are unfamiliar with today. Scholars in Ireland told an investigator there was no "tuppence" as Bridey had claimed, but he later found evidence of its existence between 1797 and 1850. Bridey was born in 1798 and died in 1864. (16)

Ruth's spontaneity in recalling aspects of Bridey's life lends credence to her testimony. When Mr. Bernstein repeated a post hypnotic suggestion, Ruth danced the morning jig and yawned at the end of it. After her performance she was stunned.

It is unlikely Mrs. Simmons read about or saw a movie on the life of Bridey Murphy, for it was the quiet life of a childless housewife. If the past life recollection were based on a story it is difficult to believe it would include an after-death episode as Ruth reported, where Bridey's spirit stayed Earthbound with her lonely husband.

The information in Betty Riley's dreams of a past life in which she died in the Great Fire of London was verified by Lucy Huie, a member of a dream study group. She had visited England and knew its history. Mrs. Riley could answer Mrs. Huie's questions about England even when they had nothing to do with her dreams. She knew who was king at the time the old woman in the dreams had lived, the year, the names of streets and theaters, and specifics relating to clothing, furniture, and buildings.

Mrs. Huie was able to verify as historically accurate over 100 details from Betty's dreams of seventeenth century England. Most of the information came from a rare book collection at

Atlanta's Emory University, which was located in a locked room only accessible to Emory alumni. Mrs. Huie used more than sixty books in her research.

In October of 1978 Mrs. Huie took Betty to England. On the ride from the airport to Victoria Station Mrs. Riley experienced longing and sadness, but she felt joy at the same time. She whispered she was home.

Betty recognized such sights as the Tower of London and described an underground passage from it to Whitehall Palace. When the two women visited the Banqueting Hall, the only part of old Whitehall remaining, they were given brochures detailing its history. The material claimed the Banqueting Hall was the same as it had been in the seventeenth century, but Mrs. Riley knew something was wrong. She remembered the door as oak, the single throne as double, the crest over the platform as having two lions instead of one, and the hardwood floors as black and white tile. She recalled tapestries hanging on the wall and diamond-shaped, rather than square windows.

After much searching Mrs. Huie located an old history book with a picture of the Banqueting Hall in Charles II's reign. It was just as Mrs. Riley had seen it, with the tapestries, diamond-shaped windows and black and white tile floor. When she investigated it, Mrs. Huie found the present hall represented the room after the great fire. Mrs. Riley had envisioned it the way it had appeared before the fire, when the old woman was alive.

A Psychological Stress Evaluator Test (voice analysis) was given to Mrs. Riley, and she was judged to be telling the truth. She said she had neither done reading nor research on the place or time in her dreams of England, and she hadn't seen a movie or television program in that setting. No one had described the events in her dreams to her when she was a child. Under hypnosis she claimed she had received her information by taking the soul back in time. She felt her memories might have been triggered by illness and by watching "Upstairs, Downstairs" on television. (17)

I was impressed when I read about Bridey Murphy and Betty Riley, but Jenny Cockell's experience was even more convincing.

She traced all ten of Mary Sutton's children, and she made contact with the six living during her search. Her book, ACROSS TIME AND DEATH, (18) is aptly named as Mary's maternal love transcended time and death when Jenny worried about the children left behind in the 1930's.

Love and guilt drove Mrs. Cockell on her odyssey after her own children were born. Their love strengthened her maternal feelings, and she had to find the children deprived of their mother at an early age. Jenny's need to seek them grew in her thirties, as she approached Mary's age when she died.

Mrs. Cockell started her search in her native England by comparing a detailed map of Malahide, Ireland, where she believed Mary had lived, with one she had drawn before obtaining it. Her simple map proved accurate, and as it supported her dreams and memories, the drawing encouraged her.

To substantiate her experiences, and to learn more about Mary, Jenny submitted to hypnotic regression. During the sessions Mary came to life. Jenny smelled the grass on the slopes and breathed the fresh air. Mary wore the long dark wool skirt Jenny remembered, and Mary's home appeared as Jenny had recalled it. She gave Mary's husband's name as Bryan and their surname as O'Neil, but they didn't feel accurate.

Frustrated with the slow pace of the regressions, Jenny sent letters to the O'Neil residents of the Malahide area. She was desperate. Memories of Mary's life came on a daily basis, as they had in childhood, and Mary's separation from her children tormented Jenny. An obsession with finding them consumed her.

Unsuccessful in tracing Mary with the suspect surname, Jenny decided to find the family by locating the cottage in her dreams. She went to Malahide and found a familiar church and butcher shop, but the cottage was in ruins.

When a former neighbor of the family supplied Mrs. Cockell with their correct surname, Sutton, a priest located six of the children's baptismal records. Later, birth certificates and Mary's death certificate were found. A Dublin newspaper published a letter from Mrs. Cockell, listing the children's names and birth data. Jeffrey, one of the sons, called and gave the addresses and phone numbers of two of his brothers.

In time Mrs. Cockell was able to account for all ten of Mary's children, and she has met the five who are still living. (Jeffrey died before the reunion.) Since then her worry and guilt have dissipated, and she knows the peace that eluded her before locating her past-life children.

Helen Wambach approached the study of reincarnation in a different manner, which was meaningful to me as a fellow psychologist. She believed she had led the life of an eighteenth century Quaker preacher. Mystical experiences, including de`ja'-vu, were involved, but she attempted to be scientific, refusing to endorse any belief on faith alone. Dr. Wambach's memories connected her with John Woolman, the Quaker preacher. They disturbed her, as she hadn't been interested in the occult or psychic phenomena before she saw Woolman's book, but she knew it had been her book.

As she thumbed through it, she became the man on a mule, traveling across a field with the book propped on the saddle before him. She was aware of what would come next before she read it, and when she saw the author's name she knew she had been John Woolman. (19)

In an attempt to find a rational explanation for her experiences and those of others, she began regressing people to their past lives by hypnosis. Her best subject was Robert Logg, a retired businessman. He recalled fourteen lives, including one into which he was born within four months of his death as a nineteenth century engineer in an Egyptian cotton mill. After rebirth he met the captain of the British ship the DOLPHIN, and when he was fourteen they sailed the world together.

Wambach discovered an English ship named the DOLPHIN in the British registry for the time period Logg claimed he traveled on it. She was able to verify some of the information from Logg's Egyptian lives, including the hieroglyphics he drew while hypnotized. (20)

Although the lives of Robert Logg and others were substantiated to some degree, Dr. Wambach's overall strategy for study was not the examination of individual cases, which are difficult to verify. She preferred to hypnotize groups of people, regressing them to three different lives in different times and places. Their fourth experience was the recall of the period between lives, before birth into their present lives. Wambach studied the past lives of over one-thousand people.

Participants filled out a questionnaire after each regression, revealing the time period chosen, and the sex, personal appearance, and clothing of the person recalled. They also answered questions on food, utensils, money, landscape, climate, and activities as children and adults. Participants gave their age at and cause of death, as well as their feelings about it. Some mentioned Karmic connections, naming people in their current lives they knew in a past life.

An analysis of Wambach's approximately 1100 data sheets showed agreement with historical patterns. She counted her participants' lifetimes in each time period and found them in harmony with estimates of the world's population at different times. Wambach's data illustrated the doubling of the world's population between 400 and 1600 A.D.. Many more lives occurred in the twentieth century than earlier. There was a big jump from 1100 to 1500 A.D., and a steep incline from 1500 to the present. (21)

The sex ratio was as expected. An average of 49.4% of the lives were female, and 50.6% were male. (22)

Before 1900 infant mortality was high, and life expectancy was lower than it is today. Wambach's data supports this, with fewer people reporting they died in early childhood and more people claiming to live longer in the twentieth century than in previous time periods.

60 to 77% of Wambach's participants' lives were lower-class; less than 10% were upper-class. (23) The number of middle-class lives varied, depending upon the historical period. Most of Wambach's subjects didn't claim lives as famous people. All of these things seem plausible, as most of the world's people have been poor. Few were rich or famous.

The details of life in the various periods of history were substantiated. Pre-Civil War currency was correctly described as larger than current bills, dark green on one side and lighter green on the other. Participants said their early American forks had two tines, accurate for all but the upper classes, whose forks had four tines.

Reports of clothing, coins, food, and utensils for the same period were consistent and could be verified in many cases. As an example, participants' reports reflected the known use of materials for plates throughout history. Wood and other primitive containers were used by most people from 500 B.C. until 1250 A.D.. China and pottery use rose sharply after 1250 A.D.. (24)

A criticism of hypnosis is people create stories under its influence. Wambach didn't feel her subjects fantasized about such mundane things as currency and eating utensils.

Wambach's data on death experiences corresponds with the near-death research of Kubler-Ross and Moody. At death 49% of Wambach's participants felt calm and were at peace. 30% described a feeling of release, and 20% floated over their bodies. Some experienced sadness over leaving their loved ones in mourning. Overall, death was considered a blessing. (25)

I believe the evidence for reincarnation is compelling, and there is no other satisfactory explanation for my link with Amanda Randall. However, the existence of past lives may never be proven for many. Skeptics gain support from such sources as Moody's COMING BACK, (26) where the mind seems to construct dramas that exist at the unconscious level and past lives are like personal myths. Dr. Moody gives the example of a patient who had suffered from high blood pressure for years. When she was regressed Anne described the circumstances of her death in an Egyptian life, in which she tried to escape an invading horde slaughtering fellow citizens. The pressure to get away seemed overwhelming to her, but when she later discussed her panic she found relief. After several regressions and psychotherapy Anne's blood pressure improved, and she needed less hypertension medicine. Since regressions affect only psychosomatic diseases, Moody concluded many past-life stories obtained during hypnosis have roots in difficult relationships or hidden neuroses in a present life. However, his findings might be interpreted differently. The troubled relationships and neuroses could have originated in past lives, and the individuals chose to reincarnate to resolve their problems. Mary Sutton failed to stand up to an abusive husband, and in her youth Jenny Cockell would walk away rather than confront an aggressive person. Her father was violent. Later Mrs. Cockell learned to express herself before angry people.

In an upcoming chapter traits Amanda and I have in common will be discussed.

Chapter Four

Helga, White Cloud, John and Mary

Three weeks after Dr. Danfield's life reading, in April of 1979, Mr. Taylor and I had the last hypnotic session before I moved to Michigan. We reviewed the lives of Anna, Helga, the fifteenth century farm woman, and White Cloud. I was pleased to discover two other lives.

After reliving the spaceship crash in which Anna, Mohari, and their children died, Mr. Taylor asked me to go backward in time, stopping when I sensed another life. Seconds later I detected a new identity, and Mr. Taylor asked me who I was.

"The name Helga comes into mind. A blonde with pigtails. Braids. In a blue outfit with a white cap."

Mr. Taylor: "How old are you?"

"Twenty-five."

"Where do you live?"

"Germany."

"Do you know what town?"

"Fussen? I think."

"What do you do?"

"I'm a housewife."

"Do you know what year it is?"

"Around 1450, I think."

"What does your husband do?"

"'E's a farmer. We work on the land. We work for. . . a prince."

"Do you enjoy your life?"

"It's all right. It's not the best life, but at least we have enough to eat. We raise pigs. We have chickens. We grow grain, grow wheat. It's very hard work, very backbreaking.

Mr. Taylor: "Do you have any children?"

"Two. A girl and a boy."

"What are their names?"

"Helga. I named the daughter after myself. Johann. It's a boy's name. The boy's about ten, and the Girl's about seven."

"You must have married young."

"Yes. My mother was afraid if I didn't marry young something bad would happen to me. Because of the **princes** (said with disdain) and the . . . army. So I got married young to a man about ten years older."   "One of my sisters was raped when there was a war going on and the soldiers were coming through. And she never really recovered. She had mental problems since then. So my mother did not want that to happen to me. So she wanted to whisk me off to some **farm** where I wouldn't be as visible."

"'Cause we lived near a highway, near a road that was traveled by a lot of people. My mother had a store. We sold all kinds of things, like rope, for example. And some food. My mother used to bake bread, and we'd sell it to strangers on the highway. Sometimes they stayed at our house too. That was another reason why my mother wanted me to leave. She didn't trust some of the **guests** that we had."

"But it's been a good life even though we've had wars going on, and a lot of times the men have to go off to fight. They leave the women alone. There are bands of other men who come and rape the women. (Helga raises her voice.) Sometimes they are killed. And sometimes the children are killed. But I have not had that happen. We have not had that happen in our area, at least for a long time, ever since I could remember. It's relatively peaceful around here now. But other parts of the country are at war."

"I just go about my every day life. Grinding up the wheat to make bread and then baking the bread. Tending my vegetable garden. Taking care of the children. I am expecting another one. I'll probably have three or four children. Most people have quite a few children around here. A lot of women have eight children before they are finished. That's just the way life is."

Mr. Taylor: "I want you to scan your memories of this person. I want you to remember all of these things. When I awake you later you will have full memory of everything you've experienced. Now we're gonna go forward in time to your very last memories in that life."

" I'm an old lady. I must be in my sixties or seventies. I've got gray hair. I look very worn and tired. I've had a busy, hard-working life. I have three of my children at my side. All together I had six. One died very young, of pneumonia, I think. The other two are sons, and they are working in the field. Two of the ones with me are daughters; one is a son. This son is a trader. He travels all over the country selling things like a peddler. He is sort of like my mother. She liked to sell things."

"So here I am at my death bed I suppose. My children are bathing me. I feel very hot, very feverish. They are calming me, consoling me, saying everything's going to be all right. I know it's not. I know this is my death bed, and these are my last hours."

Mr. Taylor: "I want you to go forward, to that point shortly after death."

"I'm at the graveyard looking at the freshly dug grave where I was placed."

"How do you feel?"

"I feel good. I feel about the same as I felt (while alive) except I'm not feverish any more. But I didn't mind dying. It was a release. It was a hard life of toil that I had gone through until the time I took to my death bed. These days people have to work hard because it's the only way to survive. I think I baked bread two days before I died."

"I didn't spent much time lingering over death. I just went to bed and died in a few hours. Maybe that was the best way, so I wasn't a burden to anybody. I didn't suffer a great deal. So now I just feel released."

"They had a nice funeral celebration. They had a funeral at the church, and then my daughters cooked a big dinner for the family. And afterwards they sang and danced. Death wasn't as sad an event as it is some places. People just pass on, and that's a thing to be expected. Why should people be sad about it? It's just part of life."

"Now I feel good. Shortly I will leave the gravesite and visit my daughters and see how they're doing. My husband died about ten years before I did. My children all have their families now, and I guess they are happy. I hated to leave them in a way, but I'm an old lady, tired of living and working. I've been a drudge. It's been a hard life. . . . . So what can I say?"

Because I had given neither Helga's maiden nor married name, it was not possible to verify her existence with a record such as a church notation of her baptism or marriage. In my research on Germany I did find facts which supported statements she made.

Helga's appearance, with blonde braids, a white cap, and a blue dress, (Under hypnosis I said "outfit", but I had the image of a long blue dress.) reminded me of that of a Dutch woman. I was surprized when I found the town of Fussen is in southern Germany, not near the border with the Netherlands. In looking at the costumes of many European countries I discovered white caps were common, and I imagine many women in the fifteenth century wore dark clothing while working, so Helga's dress was probably accurate for her time and place.

The town of Fussen was chartered in 1294 A.D.. (1) It grew up around an abbey. I visited the area in August of 1970, to see Neuschwanstein Castle, and it was the most enjoyable experience of my European trip. The day was sunny, and the castle and its surroundings--the snow-capped mountains, the lush forests and the clear blue lake--were lovely. I felt I belonged in that beautiful place, and perhaps at a deep level my visit triggered memories from long ago. Southern Germany is the only region in Europe I yearn to see again, perhaps because it had once been my home.

In Munich I bought a dirndl, a German national costume, which I felt I needed. It includes a dark green dress with orange lacing and an orange apron as well as a puffed sleeve white blouse. The bottom of the skirt is embroidered with orange, purple and white flowers. I have received many compliments on the outfit, and it has been a part of my wardrobe for over twenty years. I wonder if Helga wore a dirndl.

Her mother ran a store, and it probably did well in Helga's youth, as England and France fought the 100 Years' War until 1453. To avoid the conflict merchandise going north was diverted from the Rhone valley to the eastern Alpine passes. Commerce was also helped by the wars between the Italian city-states at that time; southern German merchants served as middlemen between Italy and the rest of Europe. (2)

It must have been a shock for Helga when she married a peasant and began working a farm owned by a prince. Most people in medieval Europe lived on the land, and life was hard. In southern Germany it was especially difficult in her time, because of a labor shortage caused by the plague and people moving to the cities and towns. Landlords demanded more services of the remaining peasants, and they were heavily taxed. Some peasants rebelled, including those in Rottweil, (3) less than 100 miles from Fussen. The fighting occurred in 1420, shortly before Helga was born.

Helga lived at the end of the middle ages, in a time of change and turmoil. Nobles battled for their rights and territory, and the movement of peasants into the cities caused friction between the municipalities and the princes.

Part of the reason for the turmoil was the lack of a strong central government; the German monarchy was weak. In Helga's youth Sigismund ruled, and toward the end of his reign he spent little time in the country. (4) The Hussite Wars raged then, and Sigismund failed to stop the conflict. The church finally made a settlement with the rebels in 1436. (5)

Weak government also contributed to general lawlessness. Provincial knights formed leagues against local princes or cities, and many knights became highwaymen. The crime and turmoil of the age explains the circumstances of Helga's life. Her sister had been raped by a soldier (or soldiers). Men were recruited throughout the country to fight the Hussites in Helga's childhood. A large army invaded Bohemia, not far from Fussen, and many men probably came through the town on their way to and from war. In order to protect Helga, her mother arranged a marriage to a peasant; the girl would be less visible on a farm than in a market.

When Helga was 25, in 1450, there was no major war in her part of Germany, but the "Zurich War", a civil conflict in nearby Switzerland, ended that year. The Hapsburg family lost the last of their Swiss land as a result. (6)

Helga said it was "relatively peaceful" in her area in 1450, but other parts of her country were at war. It was likely only comparatively peaceful, as robber-knights roamed the country, victimizing merchants and attacking villages. No wonder Helga's mother distrusted the lodgers at her home.

During most of the remainder of Helga's life (between 1455 and 1485) her country was externally at peace but in internal turmoil. As she lived between the time of Jan Hus and the Reformation, Helga saw the Roman Catholic church decline. Hus, a religious reformer, burned at the stake in 1415, and his followers attacked orthodox priests and churches, marking the beginning of the Hussite wars, which did not end until 1436. (7)

In the late middle ages corruption in the clergy was widespread, and many priests failed to perform their duties. Pious Christians turned away from them, finding comfort in mysticism and in lay groups who practiced a simpler, undogmatic religion. (8)

The mystics who flourished around the end of Helga's life might have influenced her. She lacked a fear of death, considering it part of life and to be expected. An orthodox Catholic might have feared eternal damnation for her sins, and there are many in the Catholic faith. I had expected Helga to at least show surprise when she wasn't confronted with evidence of Heaven or Hell after her death. She mentioned nothing of a religious nature. Her only concern was leaving her family.

Life in Germany at the end of the middle ages, with its civil and religious turmoil, was difficult, especially for peasants like Helga and her family. Burdened by heavy taxes levied by both church and state and by high inflation, they worked very hard for little reward. This explains why Helga resented the princes and considered death a release.

It amazed me people danced after Helga's funeral, but in the fourteenth and fifteenth centuries dancing was a craze. "...churchyards, monasteries, and church porches were at times used indiscriminately as public ballrooms." (9) Perhaps this was a fitting end for a woman who had found joy in life despite its hardships and accepted death as a part of it.

After Helga's death Mr. Taylor asked me to move forward in time until I found myself in another life.

" I see a forest. I see a tall, straight man with a black braid down his back. One feather in his hair. His name is White Cloud. He is a just, good man. He tries to be a peacemaker between Whites and Indians of his tribe and other tribes. It is 1542. He is maybe eighteen or so."

Mr. Taylor: "Are you looking at him, or are you him?"

"I'm looking at him."

"All right. Look down and tell me what you see."

I laugh. "I **am** him. I have a skirt on, made of deerskin, with fringe. I have a bare chest and teeth in a string around my neck. I have on moccasins. Leather moccasins with fringe and feathers."

"I like to look at the sun. I like the tanning rays. I like to get brown. I'm proud of myself. I like my muscles. I like to use them. I like to hunt and fish. I like to make tea out of acorns?"

"I also like to help people, to counsel them when they're feeling badly. I am becoming the tribe medicine man in a way. But I am too young to be the medicine man. I seem to have a talent for this. I like to help people. I like to gather herbs in the woods and give them something when they are feeling badly, and to talk to them when they are troubled."

"I like a white woman at the settlement, at the French settlement. She has beautiful black hair. She is very fair. But I don't know if she would have me because I am an Indian, and there is much prejudice against our kind. But she doesn't seem to be as prejudiced as the rest. Even though they appear to be friendly, outwardly, to me and to some of my kind, I don't think they consider us to be their equals. I think that they consider us dirty savages. Sometimes I've heard that term used."

Before the regression I had told Mr. Thomas about Dr. Danfield's reading. I emphasized White Cloud's frightening death; he had been killed by eagles. This supports my life-long bird phobia. Concerned about my feelings, Mr. Thomas didn't lead me through the death scene.

Although I was unable to verify the existence of White Cloud from reading histories of the eastern Indians of North America, I found some material of interest.

Before White Cloud was born, Hiawatha, an Onondaga chief, preached brotherhood among his people and the Mohawk, Seneca, Cayuga, and Oneida tribes in what is now New York state. (10) These Five Nations formed the Iroquois League, which had an unwritten constitution and called for arbitration rather than violence when tribes clashed. All tribes had to agree to war against a tribe outside the league.

I wonder if Hiawatha influenced White Cloud. They both pursued peace. Hiawatha took on the difficult task of uniting the fierce, independent Iroquois, but White Cloud went a step further when he tried to make peace between the Whites and Indians. History books differ as to the exact time Chief Hiawatha lived, but the ENCYCLOPAEDIA BRITANNICA (11) says it was around 1450. White Cloud lived about 100 years later near Niagara Falls, in Iroquois territory.

During my life reading Dr. Danfield found a white-skinned woman liked White Cloud very much. In the above regression I mentioned a fair woman White Cloud admired. She was supposedly from the French settlement, but the first French woman did not come to eastern North America until 1610. (12) She and her husband went to live in Quebec City, founded by Samuel de Champlain in 1608. Unless there was an unknown white settlement in or around New York in 1542 White Cloud couldn't have been acquainted with the woman in the regressions.

I was able to find support for two pieces of information in the White Cloud regression. Eastern Indians did make a brew (White Cloud said "tea".) from acorns, and the Indians were known as **sauvages** to the French, as were other non-Christians. Despite this the French respected and cared for the Indians to a greater degree than either the Spanish or the English. (13)

White Cloud's death helps explain feelings that were difficult to understand before the regressions, particularly my rage near Niagara Falls, when I had the impulse to push a young tour guide off a cliff. Before we left Michigan for the south Nat had taken me to see the falls. The young woman's attention to my husband angered me, and when she walked to the edge of the precipice I withdrew into the woods. Shaken, I sat on a stump to regain my composure. After the regressions I realized White Cloud might have been killed at that spot, when other Indians tied him near an eagles' nest. My rage had surprized me, but from the beginning of our private tour on that stormy day I had felt tense, uneasy.

My intense fear of birds of prey may stem from White Cloud's death. However, my phobia can be accounted for by experiences in my present life. I learned to dislike birds at a tender age; chickens pecked at my bare feet as I roamed the back yard in my walker. While gathering eggs with Grandpa I turned away as a hen pecked his hand, drawing blood.

When hawks flew over the brooder coop yard, where feeding young chickens were easy prey, Grandpa shot at them. I didn't like his gun--its loud sound startled me, and I didn't think he should shoot animals.

One spring morning I saw a hawk circling the brooder coop, where chicks roamed outside. I have to save them, I said to myself as I ran to Grandpa's door. Maybe he'll miss the hawk and only scare it away. He had missed before.

Grandpa rushed out of the house with his rifle and pointed it at the sky. I put my hands to my ears and closed my eyes. "Bang!" I squeezed my eyes.

"I got him!" Grandpa shouted.

Opening my eyes, I saw him run toward the kill. "I don't want to see it," I whispered running home.

But I couldn't help seeing it upon my return to Grandpa's yard that afternoon. He had nailed the hawk's carcass to the door of the old milk house, not far from the chicks. Looking at the bloody hawk, its wings spread wide, made me cringe. Grandpa said he had done it to scare away other hawks, but I was sorry for the bird, sorry I had told Grandpa when I saw it in the sky. I ran home crying. It was my fault, and some day a hawk might attack me to get even.

This experience was so painful I didn't recall it until recently, when I read a similar story which triggered the memory.

My love of nature, particularly of the woods and water, may be related to my life as the woodland Indian who lived near Niagara Falls. As a child my favorite place on the farm was the woods. The air was nearly always fresh, and there were floral, mossy, and earthy scents. The summer breezes were soft, and birds chirped in the trees, flying from one to another. Insects hummed, but often there was silence, peaceful silence. This was White Cloud's environment, and we both appreciated it.

After the White Cloud regression I recalled the lives of John, an eighteenth century sailor, and Mary Senze, a nineteenth century farm woman.

Mr. Taylor: "Going forward. Tell me when you're into another life."

After a few moments I replied: "I see a man with a duffel bag. I think he's a sailor. I think he drowned in the sea. But I can't get too much on him. He seems elusive."

"Tell me what you're wearing."

"I have old homespun clothing on, brown, I think it is. A bag over my shoulders. I'm throwing the bag into the sea, and it looks like I'm going to jump into the sea. (I don't like this life very well. I don't know. I have a bad feeling for it.) So I get onto the ship deck, and I jump into the sea."

"Let's go back one year. Tell me what you see."

"The man is going to the sea. He is. (I should say I. I find it hard to get inside this man. I don't know why, but I just feel . . .)

He's leaving. John is leaving for Europe, I think, on a clipper ship. I think the year is 1750, or somewhere around that.

"How do you feel?"

"He doesn't, I don't, get along with my wife. She's a pretty blonde wife, and (sigh) she likes to be friendly with other men, which I don't like at all. I don't want to fight with her. I just don't want to have anything more to do with her. I'm just going sailing. And I guess my ten-year-old son can take care of himself. He's not helpless. He can work with the sailors fishing near the shore. I've taught him to do that. So he can probably make a living for himself. Whatever she wants to do is up to her. If she wants to take up with one man or another, that's up to her. I just kind of want to wash my hands of the whole thing."

"What port are you leaving from? Where do you live?"

"I'm leaving from Boston. I live near Boston. I have been a farmer for years, but now I want to go fishing. I want to go on a ship. I want to see some of the world, and I want to get away from my wife. She embarrasses me. She goes to the bars, and she finds men, and I feel like a fool."

"All right. "We won't stay there. We'll leave John and go forward in time, carefully so we don't miss anything."

After a minute or two I sense another life.

"I am Mary, Mary Senze. I'm a farm woman. My life is dreary."

"Where is this farm?"

"In Pennsylvania."

"How old are you?"

"Forty-five."

"Do you have children?"

"Yes, I have four children."

"How do you feel?"

"Tired. Worn out."

"What year is it?"

"It's in the later half of the 1800's. 1865, or something like that. I don't know. It must be later. The Civil War has been fought. One of my sons was in the Civil War, but he came back all right, thank God. My husband died about ten years ago."

"Do you run the farm?"

"Yes, with the help of a man who is crippled. He does a lot of the work for me, even though he limps. And my twenty-year-old son has helped me ever since he was back. I have a fifteen-year-old daughter too. She is getting to the point where she is interested in men, so I have to find her a husband if I can. Keep her out of trouble."

At this point there is a tape malfunction, but I recall admitting to Mr. Taylor my youngest child was fathered by a peddler, after my husband was gone. Mary Senze died peacefully; she was about sixty-five at the time.

There is little verifiable information from the John and Mary lifetimes, but the accounts of their lives seems logical. John was probably correct in indicating he wore homespun clothing. In 1750 Boston was part of a British colony, and to avoid the expense of fabric from the mother country colonists made their own cloth from linen and wool.

John was supposedly leaving for Europe on a clipper ship. The first true clipper ship was not built until 1845, but the term "clipper" was used loosely to refer to very fast sailing ships. Baltimore Clippers were really schooners. (14)

At the time of the regression Mary recalled the civil war. It ended in 1865, and she realized she was speaking after that date as her son had returned from the war. It would be difficult to trace her since she didn't give the name of a town or county in Pennsylvania.

Dr. Stevenson is skeptical of the information on former lives obtained through hypnosis. The influence of the hypnotist is one problem with this method of learning about past lives. I believe the story of Anna and Mohari was created in part to please Mr. Taylor. Both Anna's husband and Mr. Taylor's first wife were alcoholics, and I sensed he enjoyed the romance between Anna and Mohari. He also seemed interested in Mohari's ship. Anna should have been afraid of it when she first saw it, but she showed no emotion, suggesting a fantasy. Mr. Taylor exerted little influence on the accounts of the other incarnations. We spent only a short time on these lives, which yielded little more than basic information, such as where and when the individuals lived, their occupations, their families, and how they died.

The four personalities seemed distinct. White Cloud had a terse communication style: "...I like to get brown...I like my muscles. I like to use them. I like to hunt and fish..."

Those are the words of a simple man, but his last observation shows intelligence and perception: "...I don't think they (the French) consider us to be their equals. I think they consider us dirty savages. Sometimes I've heard that term used."

In contrast to White Cloud, Helga maintained a lucid communication style throughout the regression. Like White Cloud she distrusted some people, in her case princes, but both of them projected a positive attitude toward life in general.

John, the farmer turned sailor, seemed a bitter man, one who pushed people away from him. He was articulate throughout the regression, but one part of his conversation resembled White Cloud's: " ...now I want to go fishing. I want to go on a ship. I want to see some of the world, and I want to get away from my wife." Here several of his thoughts began with **I want**, whereas White Cloud's began with **I like.**

I don't think John's life is a fantasy. I am good at spinning stories, and I could have easily created the tale of a sailor visiting exotic ports. Instead, I had trouble getting into John. My distressing childhood experience of watching a man jumping overboard in a movie on television may have triggered the memory of John's suicide. It was as if I were drowning, and the experience was so frightening I had to leave my grandparents' living room.

Perhaps because her life was that of a typical farm woman, and I grew up on a farm, I got into Mary with ease. Like Helga, she was tired, and she seemed resigned to her life. Unlike Helga, she lacked vitality, and she was not sure of the year at the time of the regression. Her husband's death and the devastation of the Battle of Gettysburg, fought in her state, might have affected Mary mentally. It is interesting Mary shared my great-grandmother's maiden name, Sentz. In the 1850's part of my family came to the United States from Germany, but to my knowledge none of my relatives settled in Pennsylvania.

The regressions in this chapter illustrate different mental levels. In White Cloud this is especially clear. He said he liked his muscles, to hunt, to fish, and to gather herbs. Here a primitive part of the psyche was tapped. When he confided the whites didn't consider him or his people their equals a higher level of thought came through.

Another level came from me (Marie) when I attempted to get into the incarnations and translate their experiences into modern terms. The most obvious indication of my influence is the fact no German or Indian language was present in the regressions to the lives of Helga and White Cloud. More subtle is my use of the terms "I guess" and "I think" in the regressions. I often use them in everyday conversation.

I found it very difficult to assume John's identity, as expressed: "...**it looks like** I'm going to jump into the sea. I don't like this life very well...I have a bad feeling for it."

Here the hidden observer (See chapter 2.) showed herself. On one level I was John and on another Marie, and I had trouble switching from Marie to John because I disliked him. The idea of suicide disturbs me--from my psychic readings I learned suicide is a major transgression. As it harmed the entity of which we are a part, I was disgusted with John for taking his life.

My spiritual nature is exemplified by White Cloud's peacemaking role and Helga's easy acceptance of death. During the Viet Nam War I marched for peace, and I have worked to become a more tranquil person. Helga means "holy"; the name suits a spiritual person. I like both Helga and White Cloud, and I am proud to be connected with them.

My point of view was shown in several instances. In White Cloud's speech it is evident. When he said: "Sometimes I have heard that **term** used." Marie's style of communication was apparent. There was a question in White Cloud's voice as he announced he made tea out of acorns. At the time of the regression I wasn't certain Indians made the brew.

In three of the four lives I used modern terms. Helga wore "pigtails", her mother ran "a store", her sister had "mental problems", and she thought one of her children had died "of pneumonia". White Cloud liked the sun's "tanning rays", and John's wife went to "bars".

The existence of various mental levels confuses some people, and as a result they question the validity of regressions. Humans are complex, however; we don't always think or behave in the same ways. Even highly intelligent adults sometimes act like children.

Other criticism centers on the problem of time. Helga said her son was **about** ten and her daughter **about** seven, and Mary couldn't recall the year when she spoke. Neither Helga nor John was certain of the year of their regressions. Both Helga's and Mary's husbands had died **about ten years ago**.

I believe we are only conscious of time in the normal waking state. In an altered state like hypnosis time is difficult to comprehend, and when an hypnotized person is asked to recall facts dealing with time errors result. This might be especially true for White Cloud. He claimed he knew a French woman in 1542, but the first French woman didn't arrive in North America until 1610. Unaccustomed to thinking of time the way Europeans conceived of it, it would have been easy for an Indian to give an incorrect year. Since John didn't identify himself until 1750, White Cloud could have lived in the 1600's; there is a 208 year gap between the alleged years of their regressions.

A third reason for skepticism about the past lives presented might be common elements such as both Helga and Mary living on farms and mothers' concerns about finding husbands for their daughters to protect them. This reflects reality; in the times of Helga and Mary most people lived on farms. Many marriages were arranged in medieval Europe, and it was not unusual for a nineteenth century farm woman to help her daughter find a husband. In addition, the unconscious is likely organized according to basic elements, as in Jung's archetypes. Marriage could be included among them.

Synchronicity might also be a factor in the organization of the unconscious. An example from my regressions is the similarity in the names of the towns **Fussen,** where Helga lived, and **Faison**, North Carolina, where Anna supposedly married Jake. (The town has no record of the marriage at the date I had given.)

In conclusion, I have neither been able to prove nor disprove the existence of Helga, White Cloud, John, Mary Sentz, or Anna. The information given by them does not conflict with historical facts (except in the case of the French woman in 1542) or common sense, so it is possible they existed and led the lives they claimed. This is more than I can say for my experience with a psychic, detailed in the next chapter.

Chapter Five

Synchronicity in Finding Amanda

As I had never visited a fortune teller, Marlene insisted I see one before I left for Michigan. An elderly woman invited us into her small apartment in a public housing development. Her tools were a deck of ordinary playing cards, and a small crystal ball which dangled on a chain. She also read my palm. The reader instructed me to ask the crystal ball only questions which could be answered "yes" or "no". If it moved forward and backward the answer was "yes", and if it moved left and right the answer was "no".

I felt the woman had little psychic ability, and perhaps no common sense. Although I wore a wedding ring she said I wasn't married. When I told her I was married she said my husband left the finances to me. This is not true; Nat enjoys handling the family finances.

The reader told both Marlene and me we were stubborn. After the session Marlene said the woman "had a good thing going there". Nearly everyone can be considered stubborn in some way. Marlene had little faith in the woman's powers, but she said I needed to experience a reading. We could have gone to a psychic with a reputation for accurate predictions, but Mrs. Green was difficult to see. I had heard from others that people waited in their cars for hours outside her home for a reading.

Marlene and I disagreed on the value of the pendulum. Mr. Taylor had told her it was able to transmit information from the unconscious, and she thought it was the only tool the psychic had used well. At the time I thought the woman was guessing the answers to such questions as whether I was moving in the near future, and consciously manipulating the pendulum.

When I thought about it later Marlene's point of view made sense. Targ and Puthoff's experiments with remote viewing supported telepathy. Perhaps the psychic had read my thoughts and unconsciously influenced the movement of the small crystal ball.

That afternoon Mr. Taylor did an experimental hypnosis session where I made contact with Anna's children after she had disappeared. I was born about three years after Anna had left them, so I had been Marie for most of the period we explored. It was difficult to obtain information; when Mr. Taylor called out most of the years my mind was blank. Nevertheless, I did give an account of the family's life after 1943.

While World War II. still raged Jake had taken the children to Fresno, California. He worked in a defense plant making aircraft and hired an elderly woman to care for the children. She didn't treat them well; she was only interested in her pay. Jake later married a younger woman who was a good mother to his children.

Sam, the son, had married young and fathered two children. His daughter graduated from college, and she had a daughter in 1979, the year of the regression.

Anna's daughter didn't fare well. Like her brother, she had married young, but the relationship quickly ended in divorce.

For years Sharon had supported herself by working as a waitress, but she had became an alcoholic and was working sporadically and accepting welfare in 1979. She looked unkempt and lived in a low-rent walk-up apartment. I could get no more information on her.

Before we said good-bye I asked Mr. Taylor how to hypnotize myself, and he gave me instructions. I have never done it, however, because I fear the situation will get out of control, as it did for Betty Riley. Even before reading about her the emotions I might experience concerned me. I have a tendency toward mood swings, and depression is sometimes a problem, although not severe enough to seek help. I am worried depression over the loss of Mohari or some other trauma will affect me if the regressions continue. In self hypnosis there is no one to help with painful memories.

We made a profit when our house sold, and the move went well. Our home in Michigan was older than the ranch in the south, but roomier. An upstairs and a family room had been added to the original home, which made our house the largest on the block.

I was happy to live in a Detroit suburb, not far from friends and family. Several planes flew daily between Detroit and New York, where I hoped to sell my writing. I yearned to take a writers' course to help me with the story of Anna and Mohari.

Unable to find a teaching position, I decided to work full time on JOURNEY INTO AZURE NIGHT. I focused on organizing and putting into words what had happened in the regressions, and thought about reincarnation.

Reviewing my life, it made a lot of sense. Not only did it explain my early memory of a woman dying in a hospital, but it also gave meaning to my fear of drowning. I recalled the childhood incident when I had screamed as a man on t.v. jumped into a large body of water. John, a previous personality, had ended his life by jumping from a ship, and I had been tempted to jump overboard on a trip from England to Denmark, after my boyfriend and I had parted. My parents naming their youngest child, James, after my father's uncle who had died as a young man had new meaning. Perhaps a new life had been nurtured in the same farmhouse.

Fear of driving had led to my obtaining a driver's license at the age of 26, although I had completed driver's training at 16. The feeling I would crash into something had puzzled me, as I had never been in an automobile accident or a crash of any kind. Perhaps I **had** been the victim of a space craft accident in my last life.

Now I could look at the Niagara Falls incident in a different way. Maybe the young woman I had wanted to push off the cliff had been one of White Cloud's killers. The Indian had lived in the area according to Dr. Danfield.

Yes, reincarnation made sense, and it grew on my skeptical mind. The idea appealed to me emotionally as well. It seemed fairer than what traditional Christianity taught--a person has only one chance at redemption. This disturbed me as some people seemed to have all the advantages in life, while others had few. How could everyone be judged by the same standards?

With reincarnation a person has as many chances as needed to perfect herself and to earn her way to Heaven. For those who believe the universe is ultimately just, reincarnation has great appeal.

The September after we returned to Michigan I enrolled in a creative writing class at a local high school. The teacher had worked in advertising and published a book on wine making. Mrs. Monroe had resided in Anna and Jake's city during World War II., when they lived there.

I learned the fundamentals of writing fiction and non-fiction from Mrs. Monroe. She encouraged us to try both, but acknowledged one or the other came easier for each writer. I wasn't sure whether to classify my manuscript as fiction or non-fiction, and it troubled me. I would investigate Anna's life in October, after my sister Tracey's wedding.

In preparation for my trip I had joined a local genealogical society. Proof of membership or a family relationship was necessary to obtain birth, death and other records from the New England city I would visit. A few days before I was to leave, Audrey, a long-time friend, surprized me. A genealogist acquaintance had called. She hadn't heard from him in months but was eager to see him. Audrey told him about my research, and he offered to help. When they visited the day before my trip Gordon advised the most important source for finding Anna would be city directories. He also constructed a genealogical chart of Anna's family, based on information from the regressions.

I believe Gordon's appearance is an example of synchronicity, what Carl Jung called meaningful coincidence. He thought the laws of nature and causality could not explain everything. The connection between cause and effect might only be relatively true, and other factors might be necessary to explain natural occurrences.

He proposed the triad of classical physics: space, time, and causality, be supplemented by synchronicity, an acausal factor. Jung thought the relationship of synchronicity to space, time, and causality is the same as time is to the three dimensions of space. He saw synchronous phenomena as a special class of natural events, partially dependent upon "... a universal factor existing from all eternity, and partly as the sum of countless individual acts of creation occurring in time." (1)

In my opinion a chain of synchronous events started when I met Marlene. She "happened to" sign up for my psychology class, we became friends, and she introduced me to the hypnotist, who helped me uncover the life of Anna, among others. The fact my creative writing teacher had come from the town where Anna and Jake had lived was a meaningful coincidence as well. Gordon, whom I had not seen in more than a year, had contacted our mutual friend just before my trip, and he helped prepare me for my investigation. It seemed I was involved in a mind network. I wonder if we are all connected the way our homes and businesses are linked for electricity.

P.M.H. Atwater, (2) a near-death survivor, wrote fellow survivors have seen "... a web-like substance connecting all in sight with everything else through a network of glistening threads."

Philosophers throughout the ages have taught the relatedness of all things. Hippocrates (3) said: "There is one common flow, one common breathing, all things are in sympathy."

Pythagoras's Harmony of the Spheres, which underlies astrology, expressed the idea "... meaningful coincidences are manifestations of an all-embracing universal order..." (4)

The importance of synchronicity was rediscovered in the twentieth century. Physicist Wolfgang Pauli influenced Carl Jung on the subject. Pauli's exclusion principle, which involves an acausal connection of particles, can be considered complementary to the principle of synchronicity. "Wolfgang Pauli's most famous contribution to physics involved the discovery of an abstract pattern that lies hidden beneath the surface of atomic matter and determines its behavior in a noncausal way." (5)

Pauli believed meaning exists in nature and suggested objective physics, with its cause and effect, could integrate with subjective values like meaning and equivalence. Meaning is essential to understand synchronicity.

Ferguson, in THE AQUARIAN CONSPIRACY, describes synchronicity as a web of coincidence that seems to have a higher purpose or connectedness. It fits with the holographic model. "Such meaningful coincidences derive from the purposeful, patterned, organizing nature of the matrix." (6) According to her, reality can be seen as a living matrix, every object containing aspects of the whole. Each object involves every other object and is in every other object.

Not only are objects related to one another, but matter is connected with mind. Physicist F. David Peat believes "... mind and matter are not separate and distinct substances but ... like light and radio waves they are orders that lie within a common spectrum." (7)

Before my trip to New England I began to look at life differently. I gazed at a map of the city I would visit. When it arrived my failure to find a street named Marshall Place disappointed me, but a Marshall Avenue lay near the ocean. What did this mean?

Painting the garage I looked up at an azure sky, rare in our cloudy area. Was this a sign I would find the information to complete JOURNEY INTO AZURE NIGHT?

On October 14, 1979, I flew to New York. The plane sped through the sunny sky, and as it approached the airport passengers were treated to a clear view of Manhattan and the Statue of Liberty. This excited me, and I felt confident the trip would be successful.

The crisp air, indicative of fall, invigorated me. As I waited for the shuttle plane a friendly Texan crossed my path. He asked me the purpose of my trip, and I confided in him, telling him about the hypnotic regressions. He wished me luck on my research.

When the small plane shifted it felt like a roller coaster and I became nauseous. Concentrating on the ocean, which reflected the sun in sequins of light, enabled me to reorient myself.

At the little airport a cab driver approached me. I stored my baggage and began my adventure. As we drove along Marshall Avenue a curve in the street, near the ocean, seemed familiar, although I had never been in the state before, at least as Marie.

I asked the driver to leave me to explore the area. Watching the waves beat the shore made me feel at home, but I did not linger long as a cool breeze blew from the ocean, chilling me. I must get on with my business. I saw someone in a nearby yard.

The man, raking leaves, told me he hadn't lived in the vicinity during the 1940's, but he pointed to a home where neighbors had lived for twenty years.

I rang the Crompton's door bell, and an attractive middle-aged woman in a wool blazer answered. I told her my story, and Elaine agreed to help me by asking the neighbors about Anna. Then she drove me to the airport to pick up my luggage, and on to a motel.

After unpacking and eating in a restaurant down the street, I searched the phone book for Randalls. Finding several, I began calling them, inquiring about Anna and Jake. No one had known them, but some volunteered information about other relatives. One man discussed his friendship with another Randall, who had played hockey in high school and had gone to California in the early 1940's. He had died in the late 1950's. I wondered if Jake had played hockey. I could have gotten his first name wrong in the regressions.

The next day I left the inn and checked into an hotel downtown. From there I could walk to the library and historical society, to do my research.

The town square with its luscious grass and white church was beautiful, but unfamiliar, I noted exploring the city. It was Monday, and I discovered the historical society was closed, but the old city directories should be at the library, a short distance away. Securing the 1941 directory in the vintage library, I placed it unopened on the table before me and concentrated, visualizing the names of Anna and Jake Randall. I opened the book to the "R" section and gasped. Jake Randall was there. But what's this? I asked myself. His wife was listed as Amanda, not Anna. This couldn't be her, I thought, disappointed. Then I reconsidered. But maybe her given name was Amanda, and Anna was her nickname.

I hurried to check out more directories. When I located the Randalls in the 1946 edition, for the year of my birth, I silently screamed. She's listed as deceased. She should have disappeared with Mohari!

Disheartened, but with no other leads, I decided to investigate Amanda and Jake Randall. On a map I located their address in 1941, and took a bus to Dartmouth Street.

The well-maintained neighborhood consisted of homes and small shops. I was surprised to find a liquor store at the address given in the directory, but I recognized nothing. The man behind the counter smiled as I entered. When I asked about the building he said there were two apartments, one behind, and one above the store. The AfroAmerican had owned the building only a short time; he knew nothing about anyone living there in the 1940's. Fortunately, he did know the former landlord, and he wrote down his name and telephone number.

After dinner I returned to the hotel and called Mr. Lucini. Yes, the Randall's had rented the upper apartment in the 1940's. He gave me their daughter's married name and said he thought she still lived in the area.

I had no trouble locating Amanda Jones. Her husband's name was listed in the phone directory, and she answered when I called. A friendly woman, Mrs. Jones enjoyed reminiscing about her early life. She and her brother Jim had grown up in Mr. Lucini's building. They were poor as Mr. Randall had been unemployed, then labored for the DPW during the depression. Mrs. Randall worked for a grocery store chain.

Amanda and Jake met on a trolley car where Jake was conductor. A Catholic, his first marriage to a wealthy girl of his faith, had been annulled. Amanda was a protestant of Danish descent.

Their first child, a nine pound son, was still born, strangled by the umbilical cord. Jim came next, then Amanda, named for her mother.

Jim had served in the army during World War II., and his mother was anticipating his visit when she had a hemorrhage. Amanda said her mother wanted everything perfect when Jim arrived, and she had worked hard to clean the apartment.

I asked Amanda the circumstances of her mother's death.

"I was bitter about it for a long time," she said. "If she had had better care it wouldn't have happened. She had an ulcer, but the doctors in those days . . . "

"Where did she die?"

"She was at St. John's Hospital for two days. The nuns did what they could, but the ulcer had ruptured. She died Tuesday morning around six o'clock."

When Amanda mentioned nuns I became excited. "That's amazing! When I was a little girl I saw myself as an old woman dying in a hospital bed with my daughter and nuns in the room. Were you with your mother when she died?"

"I held her hand."

"Were you wearing a scarf?"

"I may have been."

I remembered my daughter had on a scarf; she had planned to stay at the hospital for only a short time. Had I found her again? I shivered, and goosebumps appeared on my arms. If I had this was a miracle.

In further conversation Amanda told me her mother had been a kind, sweet woman, but she did nothing to distinguish herself from other women of her time. With Mohari in mind, I asked whether Mrs. Randall had read science fiction. Her mother had shown no interest in it. I desperately wanted to account for Mohari, but to Amanda's daughter's knowledge there had been no lover. Without an interest in science fiction it wasn't likely Mohari existed in her mother's fantasies. I hung up frustrated and confused, concluding I had not found the woman I was seeking. I was born at 5:52 p.m., three months after Amanda had died (at around 6:00 a.m.). If she were my previous personality how could I account for Anna, a young woman in the 1940's?

Anna and Mohari seemed real. Mohari had to exist, or I wouldn't have grieved for him, would I? Believing I had spoken the truth under hypnosis and trusting my feelings, the next day I continued my search for Anna and Mohari. On my way to the historical society I stopped at a drug store to ask directions.

A graying customer I had never met made eye contact with me and appeared frustrated when I failed to recognize him. He had heard me ask the way to the historical society and questioned what I hoped to find there. I told him I was researching a book and needed to find the city directories and any other pertinent information on the 1940's. Would the nearby university allow me to use their library? He replied the private school was inaccessible to the public and suggested I contact the publisher of the directories. I would try the historical society first.

In the society's collection of 1940's directories I found no evidence of Marshall Place, the street where Anna had lived. On Marshall Avenue about two-thirds of the lots were vacant, and one directory contained a note the street was incorrectly numbered. Three residences didn't have numbers. Some vacant property was numbered, and some was not. Had Anna lived on this street but been missed when the information for the directories was collected?

I decided to try another approach. I would visit the high school and attempt to locate Anna in the year books of the 1930's. I found the library of the city's old high school, where I looked through the books. Anna's maiden name was Garfield, but I found no Anna Garfield in the year books.

I returned to the historical society to check on Anna Garfield in the directories of the 1930's, but I found nothing.

I had exhausted my leads; I might as well go home early. Before changing my flight I went to the bureau of records and requested a copy of Amanda Randall's death certificate, just in case. Maybe I would be the only woman in America with her own death certificate.

I caught the next plane to Detroit in a confused state of mind. Could I have been both Anna and Amanda? If this were possible the world was a very different place than I had imagined, but many unusual things had happened to me. Had they been mere coincidences, or were they part of a grand design?

The next incident led me to believe the later. As I browsed in my city library I came across LOVE STORY. (8) Thinking of re- reading it, I glanced at the back cover and saw the author: Erich Segal. I blinked, scarcely believing my eyes. This was the man I had spoken with in the drug store. He had begged recognition, and I felt like a fool. I might have made more of the meeting with this famous author. But the message of the encounter was most important, wasn't it?

I tried to guess what I was supposed to learn from this synchronous event. Did meeting Erich Segal indicate I was on the right path in my research and ultimately in writing my book? Did finding LOVE STORY mean the story of Mohari and Anna was fiction? I still puzzle over these questions.

Another reminder of the trip came in the mail. When I received Amanda's death certificate it supported the information her daughter had given me, in addition to providing more facts. The elder Amanda had been born to Danish immigrants, with the surname Jensen, in the city where she had died at the age of fifty-three. Death resulted from the hemorrhage of a gastric ulcer she had suffered for three years. She had stayed in St. John's hospital for two days when she died at 5:00 on a Tuesday morning in February. After receiving the death certificate I felt disappointed. Amanda seemed a very different person from Anna, and I couldn't prove Mohari had ever lived. The two women had in common the fact they had married men with the same name; they had each borne one daughter and two sons on Earth; and each had lost an infant son. They had both lived in poverty in the same city, and they had died in the same year.

The similarity ended there. Anna's and Amanda's maiden names were different. In the early 1940's Anna was in her twenties, but Amanda was in her late forties and early fifties. Anna's husband abused her, but, according to her daughter, Amanda's did not. Anna found another man and left her husband and children. When Amanda died her children were grown, and Mrs. Jones recalled no "other man" in her mother's life.

Since I had found no evidence for the love story between Anna and Mohari I was uncertain whether to consider the book I was writing fiction or non-fiction. To be honest, I would have to call it fiction, but I had a strong feeling the story was true, and my inability to prove it frustrated me.

In time this became less important than the idea of reincarnation. Maybe Mohari had never been human, but Amanda had lived. Was I linked to her? Had I been her?

I remembered nothing of her life except her death scene, but maybe this was the way it was meant to be. I thought of the burden of remembering the people and places of a past life. The relationships, with their joys and sorrows, the conflicts, the fears. Concentration on the present with the baggage of the past would be difficult. Perhaps God mercifully "closed the curtain" between lives.

More and more I assumed there **was** a God. Maybe not the personal God of the Christian religion, but an all-powerful entity that governed the universe. I felt more comfortable with myself as my agnosticism waned, and I began experimenting with my psychic abilities.

Chapter Six

Psychic Readings, Mohari and Psi

The next three years were spent on mental exploration. I focused on psychic phenomena and began testing my visualization ability. Maybe I was living on the edge of reality; some considered my behavior "nutty" as I frequently spoke of Mohari and my past lives. Marlene and Mr. Taylor had kept me grounded by their support, and I missed it upon returning to Michigan. After my New England trip I called Mr. Taylor and told him I had found a Mr. and Mrs. Jake Randall. Their daughter had described Mrs. Randall's death scene I had remembered as a young child. However, Anna hadn't died on Earth, and Amanda's daughter couldn't account for Mohari. Mr. Taylor listened with sympathy, but he offered no explanation.

After my return from New England I began to notice the "coincidences" in my life and recorded them in my journal. On October 26, I saw a movie on television depicting a space station with 2,000 people. One of the main characters was a blonde woman named Anna. Writing the end of my book, the picture helped me create the crash scene. I hadn't known anything about the movie until the day it aired.

On October 28, 1979, I finished the first draft of my book. The next day I remarked to Nat that I missed my students. Minutes later, Kristine, a long-time friend, called asking me to teach some of her psychology classes. She had three jobs: teaching, giving therapy, and doing research, and she needed my help. I agreed to substitute.

I don't know whether my "paranormal" capabilities grew after the regressions or if I simply paid more attention to them, but they became more important. On a Thanksgiving trip to Minnesota I "saw" a deer crossing our path and warned Nat. Within the hour a doe stood on the highway before us, apparently blinded by the lights of our car. I wasn't afraid as I knew she would be there. Nat slowed down and blew the horn, and the deer ran across the road. Neither of us was surprised I had predicted the encounter.

When we returned I continued my search for Anna. In a stack of mail lay a letter from Elaine Crompton, my New England friend. She had found a Randall brother and sister who had once lived in her area. The woman had used a cottage on Marshall Point, but a rumor said she had moved to California to care for her brother. A second brother, a priest, lived in San Diego.

I called Father Randall a few days later. He knew of no Anna Randall, but he had left the eastern city in the 1930's. He indicated his Uncle might have had a daughter named Anna. Father suggested I call his sister Margaret, who had owned a cottage on the east side of the New England city.

Margaret Randall told me she didn't know an Anna Randall and never had. When I questioned her further she said she was busy.

Miss Randall was the only uncooperative person I encountered in my research. Everyone else seemed interested, and helpful. Friends and acquaintances listened attentively to my tales of reincarnation, and some shared their own unusual experiences. The wife of my husband's supervisor confided over lunch that her son, born late in her life, was precocious from infancy. A bright, obedient child, his grandmother had said he was too good to live. Bob once told his mother: "You know I really didn't want to come, but you and Daddy wanted me so bad..." Robert's early death resulting from an auto accident had devastated his parents.

A teacher asked me to speak about my hypnotic regressions to adults in a high school psychology class. After the meeting she told me her young son might be her father reincarnated. Among other things, the boy was only two years old, but he had athlete's foot. This had been a problem for his grandfather.

In January I began attending Mrs. Monroe's creative writing workshop at a local high school. She read manuscripts members submitted, and the group made comments. Then Mrs. Monroe edited the work at home. She was thorough, and the class appreciated her suggestions.

I learned Mrs. Monroe had made her home in the same section of the city where Anna had lived. They could have been neighbors. Mrs. Monroe claimed experimental aircraft had been tested in the area during World War II. Could Mohari's craft have been mistaken for a U.S. plane, or had he stationed himself in the vicinity hoping it would be?

Mrs. Monroe said I might have been unable to locate Anna's home as a hurricane had destroyed a lot of property on the Atlantic coast in 1938. This might explain why two-thirds of the property on Marshall Avenue had been listed as vacant in the 1940's.

In March and April of 1980, Mohari affected me once more. I longed for him. "No one can equal him in my mind," I wrote in my diary on March 1. "All other men leave me wanting." I imagined him as a cross between Charlton Heston and a Dane I had known who spoke perfect English. Both men appealed to me. At the time I had been reading Doris Lessing's SHIKASTA (1), the account of an alien race's guidance of human evolution. I thought the aliens might be influencing me in my dreams, as they had a twentieth century politician in the book.

An early April dream found me lying in front of Dad's old barn, near the road. Looking up I saw a huge spacecraft. Excited but afraid, I couldn't move. I wanted to run away, but the craft seemed to have power over me, communicating in a strange, wordless way. Nat awakened me in the midst of a message. Although I longed to receive it, I was happy he released me from the frightening dream.

I continued looking for Anna. She and Jake had supposedly eloped to North Carolina in 1933, when she was sixteen. I called the local library and asked in which states in the 1930's could a girl marry at age sixteen. There were three: Indiana, Tennessee, and North Carolina. I would try to get the name of the town where Anna and Jake were married when we visited Mr. Taylor the following summer.

In the meantime I continued to explore psychic territory. On my birthday, a warm day in May, I went to the Michigan Metaphysical Society's psychic fun night, which I had learned about at the society's book store. The community center was filed with practitioners of many types of divination--tarot card readers, psychometrists, a crystal ball reader, and astrologers, among others. I thought my birthday would be a good time for an astrological reading. The slender, articulate man I chose had an unusual approach: participants tossed chips with signs of the zodiac into a round box representing it.

Mr. Katroni told me I was sensitive, child-like and good at visualization, meaning what I pictured would come true. According to him not everyone had this ability. When I threw the chips into the box, asking if my book would be successful, he gave me a definite "yes" and said it was in the occult area. He revealed three magical people from the past would come into my life. I wondered if one were Mohari. Finally, he told me I am idealistic in love, and I become enthusiastic, then depressed, due to what I eat.

Thinking about the reading I admitted most of it is true. I am sensitive, and child-like because of my openness and ready acceptance of others. Idealistic in love describes me; it seems Mohari is an immortal. Most of the time I am enthusiastic, but periods of mild depression afflict me. I have never thought my moods were related to food, but it seems reasonable.

Shortly after my reading, when Mom told me Uncle Bob had no feeling in one of his arms I decided to experiment with visualization. Uncle Bob's doctor was attempting to heal his arm with an electrical current. If the treatment didn't work the arm would have to be amputated, and I couldn't let that happen. I visualized his arm returning to normal. It improved, and Uncle Bob died years later with all his limbs.

When we vacationed in the south I asked Marlene about visualization. She said it is the most powerful thing on Earth and warned me to be careful with it. Maybe I have no right to "play God" with someone else's life, even if they wish it. She and her friends once visualized and prayed another friend, severely injured in an auto accident, would survive. He lived, but he suffered so much they wondered if they should have let him go.

On another occasion she used her power to hurt someone. She would not give the details, but her efforts were successful. Her powers worked against the other person, but the evil came back to her, and she paid highly for her misdeed.

We saw Mr. Taylor twice on our trip. The first time he regressed me I reported Amanda was Anna's aunt by marriage.

I contacted Phoebie, my spirit guide. She predicted wealth, and success with my book. Phoebie advised me to continue with it, and not get sidetracked. If all went well I would travel with my books. Meeting the next incarnation of Christ in Israel, I would help him with his mission. His birth would take place in ten years, and he would be called Hiam, or a similar name.

In the second session I reported Anna and Jake were married by a justice of the peace in a small town in North Carolina. I was unsure of the name, but it might have been Fulsom. Mr. Taylor found Faison in an atlas. It is a small town in the eastern part of the state.

After the trip I felt confident of my psychic abilities, as if anything I visualized would come true. I sketched the floor plan of my dream home and felt the means would come to make it a reality.

I checked a map of North Carolina and found Faison near a major highway which goes to New England. In the library I discovered it had existed in the 1930's, and the town had a current population of 638. I had said it contained 200-300 people when Anna and Jacob were married, but it could have easily grown to 638 in more than forty years. I would write for verification of the marriage.

My obsession with Mohari continued throughout the summer. I thought of him when my sister Sandy and I saw "Xanadu". Olivia Newton-John played a muse who inspired a young man to create a night club. The movie had a magical quality, with Olivia's character appearing at will. I thought of

Mohari. Was he a muse sent to shock me out of my complacency, influencing me to create?

Perhaps an additional reading would give me more information. I attended another psychic fun night, this time with Audrey.

A clairvoyant told me light had settled over my head to show my receptivity. "Are you in a fashion career?" She asked.

"No. I'm writing a book."

"Is it about night?"

"The word night is in the title. It's called JOURNEY INTO AZURE NIGHT."

"You need to experience the life of one of the characters to add the vitality the story needs. You should get out and live. Branch out and find new friends. Meditate and write short stories before you finish the novel. You will have success with the book, but there will be rough spots, and at this time the conditions are not right for its success."

She also told me a heavy man with gray in his hair was trying to help me. This described Curt, the president of the company where my husband worked. He believed in reincarnation, and he had friends at a large publishing house. Curt had promised to find someone to read my manuscript.

I was able to fit in a second session, with a flame reader. "You do things the hard way," she said. "You're like a butterfly in a cocoon. You try to be what others want you to be. You should get more education, but someone doesn't want you to pursue it." She paused, then warned, "You will need it later, and success with the book will not come any sooner if you don't get it. The book has its own timetable."

Nat doesn't have his Ph.D., and he didn't want me to finish mine. He protested when I suggested returning to college after we moved back to Michigan. The flame reader recommended I "pet" the person opposed to my education, but I am a direct person, opposed to manipulating people.

I had decided to concentrate on my book instead of further schooling. About two weeks after the readings Curt gave Nat the name of an editor at Pocket Books and I sent him a query letter.

In the meantime I continued to search for Anna. Attempting to locate Sam Randall, Anna's son, I called Fresno, California. The phone rang a number of times. Then I thought I heard a man say "Hello." There was static. Finally a recording stated this was a non-working number.

About a week later I received a letter from North Carolina informing me there was no record of a marriage between Anna and Jacob Randall. I wondered if Anna ever existed. Perhaps I **had** been Amanda, the old woman I had remembered since infancy. Mohari might have slipped into my mind, blocking my memories of Amanda and replacing them with those of Anna. Had he sent me on a strange journey to meet people like Mrs. Monroe, who had lived in Anna's city during the war, and Curt, who believed in reincarnation and had contacts in publishing?

When Pocket Books called, asking me to send JOURNEY INTO AZURE NIGHT, mixed emotions surfaced. Happy but uneasy, I feared disappointing the publisher because of my failure to find Mohari. And Amanda and Anna seemed two very different women. I would send the proposal any way; perhaps I could forget Mohari if the book were published. The unhealthy obsession with him dominated my life. It had begun to affect my husband as well.

In December Nat dreamed of Barbon, Mohari's planet, in the solar system nearest ours. (I had thought Barbon was in a different galaxy.) He didn't remember any of the dream's content, but he wondered if he had been Mohari.

On the same day I received a letter from a Pocket Books senior editor. She thought my book should be published in hardback. Confused, I called Mrs. Monroe. She suggested I write a cover letter with Ms. Grant's comments and send it to a hard-cover publisher. Mrs. Monroe had told our class never to give up on a manuscript if an editor returns it with a encouraging rejection letter.

I wrote to Mr. Greenfield, my original contact at Pocket Books, asking if he knew anyone to whom I could submit my proposal at Simon and Schuster, a related house. He replied he knew no one and sent me a list of agents.

Uncertain about seeking an agent or trying other publishers, I decided to wait until my manuscript was nearer completion before I tried to market it. The truth was I feared my writing wasn't ready for publication. My worst fantasy was an editor accepting my proposal but rejecting the completed manuscript. I had some talent, but it needed development.

Another fear revealed itself in an astrological reading. Mark, a fellow writer, did my chart. He said my husband wanted a child, but I was afraid to have one. Mark admitted there would be a little trouble if we had a child, but it would be worth it. He detected another difficulty in our marriage. Mark told me we have enough money, but managing it is a problem. I admitted Nat tries to save all he can, while I like to spend more, although I'm not extravagant.

Mark went on, saying I am picky and either very neat or sloppy. I move furniture a lot and buy beautiful things. Most of this is true. I'm a perfectionist, but sometimes I allow myself to become sloppy. People have given many compliments on my furnishings and clothing, but I don't move furniture frequently.

Finally he told me I worked hard in college but didn't enjoy it, and I was athletic. I spent a lot of time studying in college, but I enjoyed it. Because of poor coordination I've rarely participated in sports.

Mark may have sensed my fear of having a child because it had been on my mind for several days before we met. I had read an article indicating families with mental illness also had shy, sensitive and poetic members. One of my sisters is mentally ill, and she and I were both shy as children. When I met Nat he was shy. We are both sensitive, and I am poetic. Concern over bearing a child who would become mentally ill was on my mind, but I had never discussed it with Mark.

Telepathy might have affected the reading, as Mark "homed in" on my thoughts at that time--money, decorating, and having a child. His accuracy slipped when he spoke of college experiences, which I rarely considered. In contrast, I worried about my apparent infertility. In my mid-thirties, a child would have to come soon. If we had only one offspring mental illness would be less likely than if we had several, but the risk disturbed me. As usual with psychic readings, Mark's proved accurate on most points. Except for the reader in the south, my impression of psychics is favorable. I consider them honest and helpful, but I have only dealt with those recommended by the Michigan Metaphysical Society or trusted friends. No matter which method of divination they use I believe telepathy plays a role in their readings.

Three mornings after I met with Mark a more immediate fear than bearing a mentally ill child made itself known. Early that February morning I awakened screaming. I grabbed Nat, yelling, "Ghost!" In my dream a black, shadowy figure lurked beside the bed, reaching to grab me. After the incident I couldn't go back to sleep as it might return.

Terrified of the evil being, the next day I bought a Jewish memorial candle and placed it on the night stand, near the spot where the shadowy figure had appeared. If that didn't repel it I would buy a cross, and ask Audrey, a former nun, for holy water.

Although they both came to me in dreams, the creature in black was much different from the gentle Mohari. He bore messages from his world and pressed me to write, whereas the creature had nothing to say. It seemed to be content frightening me.

Relying on the candle, prayer, and visualization, I went on with my life, although nothing seemed easy. A month after the dream my fear had subsided, but I received another jolt. One-third of the employees at my husband's office were laid off, Nat among them. The federal government would no longer fund the company's energy research, and termination was immediate.

Several times that day tears nearly came, but I couldn't cry. Would we have to sell the house? Maybe I would have to go to work, but jobs were scarce. It was like another bad dream. I nearly slipped into a trance during the evening. Frightened of losing my mind, I fought it off.

Fortunately my husband found a position at a computer company that May. I continued work on my manuscript. Mrs. Monroe told me Anna wasn't strong enough. I admitted my fear of her feelings, my inability to let her express them. If I let go would I lose myself? Writing it was a struggle, but I had faith in JOURNEY INTO AZURE NIGHT and stayed with it.

I often worked into the wee hours. One morning in May I thought of Mohari. What if he were to appear to me? I shuddered, but couldn't get the idea out of my mind. I told myself it was foolish, and to get back to work, but I couldn't concentrate. When the lights flickered my muscles tensed. Knowing I wouldn't be able to write any more that morning, I went to bed.

Three days later, at 1:00 a.m., I was working on chapter 13. Thinking of Mohari, I sensed a presence. What if the smoke alarm detected it? I would be terrified if it rang. I tried to ignore my fear and concentrate, but I couldn't. I kept thinking it would ring. Should I leave the room? No, I needed to finish the chapter. Then the alarm went off. I jumped. Our dog whimpered. Shaken, I scrambled out of my chair to investigate. Everything was in order. There was only one explanation: Mohari had come for me. No, I told myself. There's a rational reason.

The detector, located in the hall just outside the room where I did my writing, was sensitive. When someone took a shower in the bathroom at the end of the hall the steam activated it. Sometimes it went off when the tea kettle in the nearby kitchen whistled. But there was no smoke, no steam. Would a spirit have enough power to affect the smoke detector? Frightened at the prospect I ran upstairs to my husband.

In the following days I questioned myself. Maybe I paid too much attention to my thoughts and feelings. Had I gone overboard in recording them? Perhaps I lived too much in my mind. The worst example of this was in letting Mohari control me. Hoping it would break his hold, one morning I wrote a note to him: "Go to Hell, Mohari. I can't afford to go crazy."

I sought answers at another psychic fair. A palm reader said he couldn't read my palm because it was "cracked"--it had too many lines. He said I was a mess, a "nervous wreck". I should exercise, meditate, study French (in which I had expressed an interest), and return to teaching.

After that reading I needed a healer. In a quiet room, a beautiful young woman "healed" me. My hair stood on end, and I felt a "presence" above. Receiving a headache, which lasted the rest of the evening, was unpleasant, but I felt invigorated for days afterward.

Despite my precarious mental state I continued to use visualization. In June we went with Nat's mother to a race track. Because of limited funds the only horse I bet on was Carrot Kiss, in the third race. He was #7, my lucky number according to numerology, and he had a reddish coat, reminding me of my red hair. I concentrated and imagined white light around him. Carrot Kiss started last, but he won. After my mother-in-law became irritated from losing I concentrated on a horse she had chosen, and it won. I couldn't help my husband though; his horse lost despite my concentration.

Mohari haunted me throughout the summer. One day in June I nearly went into a trance. Lying in bed my head spun, control slipping away. I fought, fearing an altered state, where Mohari would rule me. Whether he was an external entity or a part of myself wasn't certain, but evil might befall me if I didn't do what he wanted--continue to write his story. This wouldn't be possible in an altered state, and in it I would be at his mercy.

At the end of summer I felt more in control of my life, and decided not to fear Mohari. His ancestors had lived on Earth, and he had been mortal. Now he was dead.

Despite this realization Mohari has never left my mind since I first dreamed of him. Who is he? I have asked myself that question again and again.

He may be a muse, like Olivia Newton-John in "Xanadu". She was a separate entity from the man she inspired to build a night club, but I believe a muse can arise from within. It may be an aspect of the unconscious, from the right brain.

The right brain, which is nonverbal, is likely in control during sleep, hypnosis, and other altered states. If dreams do not originate in the right brain, they come through it.

My dream of Mohari would be considered a breakthrough dream by Corriere and Hart,(2) which means there is a tear between the conscious and unconscious mind. The dream resembles a peak experience, providing the dreamer with a new awareness. Created from a hidden part of himself, the dream will sometimes hold him captive.

Whether Mohari was a part of me or not I felt attached to him. He could have been a separate entity for whom I had such great need that I unconsciously held him prisoner. If he is an independent being he was likely a messenger sent to inspire me to write.

He could be an angel. Sophy Burnham believes angels teach us, guide us, and give us messages. They can come as a thought or a dream or as intuition or insight. She writes in A BOOK OF ANGELS (3) one indication of an angel is "It brings a calm and peaceful serenity that descends sweetly over you, and this is true even when the angel is not seen." I can't remember a more peaceful experience than my dream of Mohari. It felt so good I didn't wish to awaken from it.

Another of Burnham's marks of an angel is a change in the person experiencing one--he is never the same as before. This is certainly true in my case. The dream changed me from a person with a rational, no-nonsense approach to life to someone open to psi influences.

One other reason I suspect Mohari is an angel is the close resemblance of his name to that of Moroni, the angel who first brought messages to Joseph Smith in 1823. The spirit directed him to golden plates buried on a hill in Ontario county, New York. THE BOOK OF MORMON (4) is based on the writing on them.

Perhaps Moroni has inspired others in addition to Joseph Smith, or there may be many messenger angels, some of whom have similar names.

Then again Mohari may be a part of myself which I cannot comprehend. Jane Roberts would depict him as an Aspect self, similar to an archetype or muse. She saw Seth, who spoke through her, dictating manuscripts, as an aspect of herself. He represented a main core of her personality and communicated through her "psychic fabric". Jane acknowledged he might be beyond our ideas of personhood, although he had a definite individuality. (5)

Julian Jaynes, in his popular book on the origin of consciousness, hypothesizes ancient man listened to messages from his right brain, which he thought were the voices of the gods. (6) Seth and Mohari may be modern examples comparable to the gods of old.

Jane Roberts, who at 34 had been an aspiring poet and novelist, wrote of one of her experiences: "A fantastic avalanche of radical, new ideas burst into my head with tremendous force, as if my skull were some sort of receiving station, turned up to unbearable volume." (7)

Her hands scribbled the words and ideas flashing through her head.   Later, in trance, she dictated the disembodied Seth's messages to her husband. Seth gave her much information about the spirit world, the nature of physical existence, and how the two relate.   He told her consciousness ends not at bodily boundaries, and both body and soul are fields of energy. We create our souls as they create us. Man has been given the ability to project thoughts into physical form, and through our desires and beliefs we make our own reality.

In 1965 Helen Cohn Schucman, a psychologist and atheist who didn't believe in the paranormal, had a similar experience. She began hearing an inner voice that wouldn't leave. From its messages she wrote A COURSE IN MIRACLES.(8)   Those successful in applying the course to their lives exchange ego connected beliefs, such as fear and anger, for God beliefs, involving love and acceptance of themselves and others. They advance from a life of pain to a life of joy and peace.

Like Roberts and Schucman, I received **inner dictation** rather than sound from without.   As I wrote the revelations Mohari had given me in the dream it was as if I were translating **in my mind**.

The messages focused on Mohari's people helping mankind in our evolution.

Lawrence Block, who wrote a monthly column for WRITERS' DIGEST, adopted a view compatible with Roberts', although he had no Seth counterpart. He wrote in 1985: "At times I think I am the source of all my work. At other times I see myself more as channel than source, conveying stories from some unknowable well--the universal unconscious ... the mind of God ... Perhaps everything we would write already exists in perfect form; it emerges on the page in one degree or another of imperfection, depending on the extent to which we are open channels." (9)

Authors Charles Dickens, Rudyard Kipling and George Eliot felt "possessed" while writing. In Eliot's best writing she thought something had taken over, making her an instrument through which the spirit acted. (10)

In another column Lawrence Block (11) discussed his relationship with the people in his stories. When he wrote about a character he became that character, seeing the world through his eyes, reliving his life. On one occasion the person about whom Block was writing a biography felt as if someone were in his head and correctly identified the intruder as Block.

Some writers, including Carolyn Chute, author of THE BEANS OF EGYPT MAINE,(12) feel their characters are real. She and her husband sometimes act out their parts.

The experiences of Block, Chute, and other writers illustrate we are open systems, mentally interacting with elements other than those we contact through our recognized senses.

Am I a channel for Mohari, a normally hidden part of myself, or is he a separate entity, perhaps an angel who awakened me, helping me to begin a writing career? He could be more than this, maybe the guardian angel I prayed to as a child, the spirit who will lead me to the next world when the time comes. Once the idea of Mohari as a separate entity tormented me. Since he hasn't haunted me for more than ten years, this fear has all but left.

Sometimes I think of a third possibility--that Mohari was, is, or has yet to be human. He and I could have been together in the past, or maybe we will have a relationship in a future life. Perhaps Anna and Mohari exist in a parallel universe.

I had read of parallel universes, but the idea was fuzzy in my mind until a "coincidence" clarified it. In May of 1991 I went to a local women's center for a mammogram. As the technician took the last x-rays I sensed my return to the clinic. That afternoon a technician called, asking me to come back the next day.

Waiting for the second mammogram I overheard a nurse and a patient discuss an anomaly. The nurse had been confused by the records of two women who had the same name but had been born a day apart. Their husbands' names were identical, and the nurse had thought they were one woman and the center had made a mistake in her birth date.

However, the patient, Jane One, said she knew of a woman with her first and last names, but their middle names were spelled differently. Jane One had become aware of Jane Two when Jane One had left the hospital after giving birth. Jane Two had left the same day, after a miscarriage. Later Jane One found Jane Two had lived in the same town, two streets away from her. Both streets began with the letter "R". I was amazed by the story, and leaving the building I discussed parallel universes with another patient who had also overheard the conversation. It reminded me of Anna and Amanda, who had similar names and whose husbands had identical names. They had lived in the same town at the same time and had each borne two sons and a daughter, their second sons dying very early in life. Had I been summoned to the women's center to learn it was possible **both** Anna and Amanda had existed, or had my returning to the center been a meaningless chance occurrence?

I thought about coincidences. What is chance? Physicist F. David Peat (13) believes reality comes from energy that is created by chance out of nothing.

Reality might be more complicated than most of us understand. Another physicist, Fred Alan Wolf, (14) hypothesizes the future can affect the present in his parallel universe theory. The mind may be a time machine sending and receiving information from the past and future. Peat believes it is possible for a person to remember a life he has not yet lived. Anna and Mohari could have "bled through" from the future, and I have yet to be Anna. Or she and Mohari could exist now in a parallel universe close to ours, but in a higher dimension in space. Wolf thinks altered states and dreams may show us the closeness of parallel worlds.

By the fall of 1981 I had decided not to focus on otherworldly concerns. Despite my resolve to make changes in my life, however, psychic manifestations continued. On November 30, and again on December 17, I felt a "presence". Both times I was alone in the house at night. It was as if someone were watching me from behind; I could feel "eyes" staring at me. The entity seemed calm, and I detected no ill will. But I felt uncomfortable, and I ordered it to leave. It left, and I don't think it ever returned.

In January authors in the professional writers' group I attended said my writing had improved. Tim, who had published a science fiction novel, remarked I am mystical, and I had taught myself to write. This was a milestone in my life; Tim's encouragement would enable me to finish JOURNEY INTO AZURE NIGHT.

Tim had also cautioned me against believing everything I had said under hypnosis. He suggested wish fulfillment and recycled dreams were involved. As an example, Jacob's abuse of Anna would justify her relationship with Mohari. I agreed I might have constructed events in Anna's life, and maybe Anna herself, because I could recall nothing of Amanda's life but her death scene. If this were true my book was fiction, but at that point Mohari's hold on me had weakened, and I could accept it.

My return to the rational world occurred slowly. The psychic manifestations continued. One night, when I was angry with Nat, we watched a documentary on the Thames River. Suddenly a flash of light lit up the television, and it went off. I changed channels, but the set remained dead. Nat worked on it, and the t.v. came back on. He said it was equipped to handle a sudden energy spurt. Because there weren't any electrical storms in the area, and we had no other explanation, I concluded my anger had turned off the television.

Synchronous events also kept occurring. During a two week period in April Nat and I went to two Chinese restaurants in separate suburbs, and they weren't part of a chain. I received one fortune cookie at each, and they both carried the message: "You will be traveling and coming into a fortune." Although the words were the same, the type on the strips of paper was different. I marveled at the "coincidence".

On an early morning in May I dreamed I was pregnant and afraid of dying during delivery. Since childhood I had feared pregnancy, thinking babies would grow in artificial wombs when I was old enough to have one.

I recognize some foreshadowing events in my life, connecting the present with the future. As a girl I loved a dark-haired paper doll named Nat. I wished to marry a man like him, and I did. Had the dream of pregnancy also been a predictor?

My life was filled with what some call the paranormal. Just before I mailed out eight query letters to publishers the names of two of them, Random House and Doubleday, came into my mind, bringing a pleasant feeling. Soon I received a letter from a Random House editor asking to see my manuscript. Doubleday didn't send a rejection either. Instead the editor instructed me to send a double-spaced letter, rather than the single-spaced one I had submitted. I dreamed of a rejection from Everest House one morning, and a few hours later it came. All of the above illustrate precognition.

In order to obtain more information on Anna and Mohari, in June I visited a writer who did hypnotic regressions. Before hypnosis we tested the tape recorder. It worked then, but when I lay down to begin the session the recorder emitted a high-pitched "scream". We used Marsha's recorder, and when we played back the transmission it sounded as if we were at the seashore, with the waves rolling in, and gulls screeching. Although a nearby window was open, the area around Marsha's country home was quiet.

Under hypnosis I spoke of Mohari and myself on Barbon, with its blood-red skies and cloud patterns reminding me of circulating dye when it is first added to water. We strolled the beach, walking on white sand.

I stood on the shore, dressed in a white amorphous gown. I was Alia, Mohari's first wife, and I thought he was beside me, but it was an illusion. The formless black thing of my (Marie's) dreams impersonated him, and I called out in fear.

"Have Mohari chase it away," Marsha commanded.

"He killed Anna!"

"No. It wants you to think that, but Mohari and Nat are your protectors."

"Do you think it is jealous of them?"

"Probably it wants you to itself."

I squirmed. "I had a horrible dream. The black thing was over my bed, about to grab me. Then I woke up. I'm afraid to go to sleep."

"What will destroy it?"

I thought about it for a moment. "I don't know."

"Let's get back to the beach. Is the thing still with you?"

"No, it melted into the sand."

"Then sand will destroy it again. When you get home put a container of sand by your bedside."

In the last minutes of the session I promised to meet Mohari at the beach in the New England city I planned to visit for the second time. He would wear a tan shirt with a thin red stripe and khaki pants. (Later I realized I had ordered my Godson an outfit with similar colors from a catalog the night before.)

I was concerned the thing might appear as Mohari, but Marsha reminded me there is sand on the beach, and what once worked against the evil entity would work again. She said Mohari would take care of me. It is likely I spend the time between lives with him, in his realm.

As Marsha had told me, Nat is also my protector. When we hugged after my dream of the thing, I felt better. My feelings for Mohari troubled me, however; I missed him deeply, often to the point of tears. At the same time I felt guilty for my disloyalty to Nat.

That night I found white sand, left over from a terrarium project, and placed it in a jar on my bedside table. When I spent the night away from home I carried a small jar of sand in my luggage. The big black thing never terrorized me again.

Maybe a friend was right when she said the thing represented my own fear. I was afraid it would possess me, perhaps destroy me. Later I acknowledged it was probably part of myself which I could control, oddly with a jar of sand.

Another friend, Audrey, didn't express an opinion on the thing, but she sensed an evil presence in the house when she stayed in the guest room overnight. Audrey also had a bad dream, but she didn't give the details. Had she sensed the same presence I had felt staring at me months before? Did it have anything to do with the smoke alarm going off in the night? I couldn't answer these questions, but all of these events had occurred within a few feet of each other. The smoke detector hung from the hall ceiling outside the room where Audrey had slept, and I felt the presence in the dining room, less than three yards from the detector. Two years later my mother heard sounds while sleeping in the guest room and concluded the house was haunted.

I feel most of the experiences in my Detroit suburban home came from within me, and others might have been affected by self-induced experiences as well. At that time I was on a quest, like a mythological hero. The hero's conscious goal may be to slay the enemy and save his people, but unconsciously he must fight another battle, between the forces of good and evil within himself.

Each of us has the potential for good and evil. Many of us emphasize the good side and downplay the darker side of our nature. Jung named the darker side the shadow. If we deny it we risk becoming its prey, for it makes itself known in unexpected ways, sometimes terrifying us.

I believe the "big black thing" was a manifestation of the shadow. As I slept it loomed over my bed, dark tentacles (fingers?) preparing to grab me. I screamed and awakened both myself and my husband.

The incident occurred after the past-life regressions, during a time of self-exploration. I had been focusing on positive psychic aspects at that time, visualizing the return of movement in Uncle Bob's limp arm, among other things.

Others have had similar experiences with their dark sides. John Cornwell, in THE HIDING PLACES OF GOD, recalls a frightening childhood experience, probably a dream. He is lying in bed on a summer evening, looking out a window, when his door opens and people hurry in with masks and scissors. As they lean over him he hears sighing and crying.

"There is a presence in the waves of sound, like an ageless, all powerful, dark being, and it gathers strength and purpose in a series of sickening, irresistible pulses. I am about to be engulfed by the monotonous rhythm which intends taking me to itself forever. This I know is the only reality, the ultimate and inescapable truth, all powerful, all evil, and without end..." (15)

Cornwell thought he had seen the devil. Largely because of his memory of the evil presence he turned to religion, carrying holy water and wearing a medal of the Virgin Mary. Later he went to a seminary, intending to become a priest.

He left the religious life because of a conflict between the religious world, where he must believe, and the physical world, where he could use knowledge and reason. Since he couldn't reconcile the two he became an agnostic.

An experience similar to Cornwell's is included in TELLING YOUR STORY: A GUIDE TO WHO YOU ARE AND WHO YOU CAN BE (16):

"A few years back I woke up in the middle of the night filled with a vast terror. I hadn't been dreaming and couldn't explain my sudden fright, except that I sensed the presence of evil in the room. I began to stare at the upper left-hand corner above my bed and I saw a creature slowly take shape like a storm cloud. It was a monkey, black but glowing around the edges, with venom and filth and slime drooling down his hairy face. He just hung there dribbling and cackling and all the time his phosphorescent eyes were riveted on me. I lay on my back trembling and whimpering. My bones were like water. He hovered there, waiting, his menacing arms waving like poisonous tentacles. I knew that he was concentrated evil and that all of his emanations were directed at me."

The author is sure the thing was not a nightmare or a fantasy, but a demon. It is not known why the thing appeared, but caged monkeys are considered degraded animals who imitate humans, and this monkey reminded the author of them. The monkey can be considered a mirror, an ugly reflection of self.

Like Cornwell, the author senses the demon will return. The demons are part of these men, as the "big black thing" is my shadow, the dark side of me.

After Jung broke away from Freud he experienced aspects of his unconscious, like the above authors. Jung journeyed deeper, however, and some thought he had suffered a nervous breakdown. During this time he uncovered the collective unconscious, with its archetypes (like the mother and father), common to all mankind. (17)

For several days in 1916 the Jung home was haunted. One Sunday morning doorbells mysteriously rang. Jung reported the whole house was full of spirits. During the next three nights, while he was possessed by spirits, he wrote SEVEN SERMONS OF THE DEAD, a cosmology of the universe, which relates how consciousness emerged out of the collective unconscious. The book is an account of the evolution of the mind, and on a deep level, mind and matter have a common origin according to Jung.

Assailed with thoughts of his world and how it related to ours after my dream of Mohari, I had a similar experience. The theme of his race helping ours kept repeating itself. For weeks afterward I felt compelled to write about his planet; Mohari had a hold on me I couldn't break. A sensation of pressure bore down on my head for months. It was slight, and I had no other physical symptoms, so I didn't see a doctor. Consequently, it was never explained, but the pressure ceased when the hypnotic regressions began.

After the past-life regressions came psychokinesis. Late at night, as I worked on the book about Mohari, I felt his presence, which frightened me. Early one morning the smoke detector sounded for no apparent reason, just as Jung's doorbell had rung with no one outside.

Physicist F. David Peat, in SYNCHRONICITY: THE BRIDGE BETWEEN MATTER AND MIND, (18) suggests the transformation of Jung's inner being was connected with the hauntings and mysteriously ringing doorbells. The psychic changes may have brought about energy transformations with the inner restructuring.

I believe psychic energy is freed when people are in crisis, either due to an emergency, as when a woman is able to lift a car to save her child's life, or in times of turmoil, such as adolescence. Where there is a poltergeist, there is often a teenager.

In a period of confusion after my regressions my anger showed itself as psychic energy in the t.v. incident. Zap! The screen lit up as if lightning had hit the set. Nat remarked the t.v. was equipped to handle power surges and switched it back on.

That was a painful time for me. Frightened of what would happen next, I retreated, staying at home when I should have gone out into the world. Reading metaphysical books, writing about Mohari, and psychic readings made the situation worse, as I became more and more wrapped up in myself. If Mohari were my protector why didn't he help me?

The mystery taunted me as I flew to New York in late June of 1982. I would deliver my partial manuscript to Random House and to an agent Marsha thought was sympathetic to new writers. Before doing business in the city I took a bus to the town where Amanda had lived. Mr. and Mrs. Crompton had invited me to stay with them, at the beach.

Their home backs up to the ocean, and they view a seascape of changing rock formations as the tide comes in and recedes. It is a tranquil place, with soft sea breezes and sparkling sunlight on the water. I was eager to visit the Cromptons.

Elaine met me at the bus station, and as she drove we discussed the mystery of Anna. She could have lived in the Crompton's neighborhood, walking the same streets and viewing the same spectacular sunsets as Elaine, but my friend hadn't been able to find a trace of her. We could only guess at what Anna's life might have been. Was she the abused wife of the regression, or had her life been distorted to justify an affair? What had happened to her children? We realized the truth might never be known.

The next day, after an outing with Elaine, I visited a private beach near the Crompton home to contact Mohari. I watched the tide come in, small waves lapping the shore. As the sun was low in the sky and I had to leave soon, I closed my eyes and visualized Mohari. When I opened them a black dog surprized me. At first I was afraid of him. When I was in high school my cousins' dog had chased and bitten me, and I had read black dogs are associated with sorcery and bizarre happenings. Nevertheless, the dog seemed friendly, so I petted him.

I visualized Mohari again, but didn't expect him to come. Perhaps the dog had appeared to inform me my wish to see Mohari was known, but he could not come. Dogs serve as companions of the dead and are linked to resurrection. (19) Since the dog was black the possible connection with Mohari, the dead lover from a past life, was even more meaningful. I stroked the dog again and again and admitted I liked him. I didn't mind when he followed me back to the Crompton home, but I was relieved when Elaine recognized him as a neighbor's dog. Maybe his appearance had no deeper meaning.

Two days later I returned to New York, handcarrying my manuscript to the Random House editor, and to the agent Marsha had met at a writers' conference. I was unprepared for my encounter at Random House. Picturing the editor as middle-aged and overweight, perhaps balding, I gasped when a tall, handsome young man appeared. As I tried to unsnap my attaché case it flew open, spilling my manuscript and other papers onto the floor. My face burned as Mr. Donaldson helped pick up the papers. Never again, I thought, the mail's safer.

Mr. Kane, the agent, worked out of a cramped office, in what appeared to be an old apartment building. He gave me a cool reception, and I wondered if my trip had been worthwhile. Before leaving New York I visited St. Patrick's Cathedral where I lit a candle at the statue of St. Catherine, patroness of the arts. By then my anger with the Catholic church had diminished, and because of my psychic experiences I knew the power of prayer and devotion. Maybe the saints, although long-dead, could influence our lives. I was beginning to think some intervention would be necessary to sell my manuscript.

In my demoralized state cutting expenses seemed important, so I decided to take a bus home rather than fly. Fortunately I met a sympathetic woman on the way to Detroit.

The former commercial artist boarded in Philadelphia, and we talked most of the night. She had come to the same conclusions as Jane Roberts in her Seth books. Amory told me I had created the Big Black Thing. It was nothing and had nowhere to go.

Returning home a dark mood enveloped me. I feared my book wouldn't be published and felt like "checking out", leaving this world, as I had many times since my dream of Mohari. I wanted to be with him. Amory had warned me of the danger the knowledge of past lives can bring, but it was too late for me. I lived with one foot in the present and the other in a past life, and felt helpless. I needed to regain control of my life and make peace with Mohari. Was that possible?

He had probably left me long ago when the pressure on my head had ceased. OUIJA: THE MOST DANGEROUS GAME (20) shed light upon what might have happened between Mohari and me. Hunt believes obsession or possession can be accidental; a spirit can become entangled in a human's aura without meaning to or knowing how to get out of it. The relationship between the entity and the person invaded can be mild or traumatic, depending upon the nature and intentions of the spirit forced to remain with the human.

Undergoing hypnosis might have changed my aura sufficiently to release Mohari. By the time my father died, more than a year after the dream of Mohari, I no longer sensed the pressure on my head or felt compelled to write about him.

The experience of physical and mental pressure is the main reason I favor the idea Mohari is an outside entity rather than a part of me. If my inkling is true, where is he? In CHANNELING (21) Jon Klimo writes psychologists have found evidence of outside energies appearing as personalities. People who lack an "aware ego" tend to bond with the entity, as in the transference process with a therapist. The outside energy force becomes the teacher, the human its student. One unable to evaluate the entity, use it, and learn from it might overvalue it, elevating it to the status of an all-knowing god.

In my case the bonding was complete. Perhaps I treated Mohari as a god, because as an agnostic, I needed one. But I went a step further. Not only did I treat his messages with reverence, but Anna's lover became mine, and my obsession with Mohari continued long after he had left me.

Klimo thinks beings from a higher frequency realm, perhaps like Mohari, can communicate with us. (22) I believe he returned to his world when I was able to let him go, but he can still communicate with me. I don't know his nature, whether he is an angel or not, or where he dwells. I understand now I can only make peace with myself.

In my troubled state I was unable to do it. I externalized my problem, telling Mohari to leave me alone. Eventually I realized he was gone. The ring of the smoke detector was my own doing, brought about by my unhealthy attachment to him.

The "presences" were likely earth-bound spirits, and my awareness of them could be considered a by-product of spiritual transformation. (23)

After her enlightenment Sophy Burnham, (24) who believes we are surrounded by angels, had psychic experiences. For a time she received messages from beyond our dimension, experienced apparitions, had dreams about past lives, and communicated with deceased friends. She served as a channel for discarnates, among them Willy, John, and Steve, who had died in Viet Nam. She had begun receiving messages from them before she met her boyfriend, who had served with them. Through her they told him death is but a passage between dimensions, and he shouldn't blame himself for what had happened to them.

I didn't want to join these spirits, but my involvement with the other world could have led to an early death. One incident brought home the danger facing me. A week after the trip to New York my husband and I ate dinner at an Indian restaurant. Feeling blue and consumed by my thoughts as we left the building, I nearly stepped in front of a speeding car. Nat pulled me back, saving me.

Shaken, I evaluated my life. Should I continue spending so much time on my book? Maybe I should have a child, or return to teaching.

Four days after the near-accident I received a rejection letter from Mr. Kane. He remarked my proposal was neither thematically nor conceptually adequate, and it didn't read like a novel. Crushed, I decided to rewrite the manuscript only after improving my writing skills. My romance writers' group would help me with a novel, which I would write for practice.

Creating the romance was a much different experience than working on the past life story. I wasn't obsessed with CANADIAN HOLIDAY, and didn't feel an outside force affecting me. I was in control, and it felt good.

Nearly a month passed before I received the letter from Random House. Mr. Donaldson wrote parts of the story were interesting, but it was not strong enough for publication. I had prepared myself for that outcome, and was not as upset as I had been about the agent's rejection. The manuscript simply needed work. I resolved never to abandon JOURNEY INTO AZURE NIGHT, if it took me a lifetime to get it into print.

I knew the psychics were right; it would take a long time for my book to appear on the shelves of book stores. I longed for Mohari and the other world and felt my life slide downward. Would I be able to hold on for several years? In the meantime what would I do with my life?

Four days later the answer came. A local college asked me to teach psychology that fall. I accepted, and when I returned to work preparing for and meeting with classes grounded me in the real world again. This marked my turning point--I had chosen to back away from the psychic world and re-enter the objective world. To survive I had to re-connect with the material realm, but I returned with knowledge and experiences that enriched my life and changed my outlook forever.

Amanda and her younger sister Anna,
about 1900.

Amanda Randall at age 51, 1944

Four generations of Marys, 1947. The youngest, a.k.a. Marie Gates, is one year old. Compare the noses with Amanda Randall's.

Amanda Jensen (later Randall) at age 20, 1912.

Marie Gates at age 21, 1967

Marie Gates and Amanda Jones, Amanda Randall's daughter,
1996. Marie, age 50, has just seen Amanda for the first time. The
author's train trip took nearly 24 hours.

Chapter Seven

Science and Divination

After my turning point I began reading books written by physicists. I needed to study the relationship between the psychic and material worlds in order to make sense of my experiences. In mankind the psychic realm mingles with the physical, and my reading helped me understand the power within us.

Everyone has psychic ability, and some who have developed it can heal as well as influence objects and events. They can perceive the future and understand the past and present in ways others cannot. Heightened perception allows them to see phenomena such as auras, which others miss. Some are able to communicate over space and time, by mysterious means.

The "magical" power within us has to do with consciousness. Philosophers and mystics have long appreciated its importance. Recently scientists have begun to follow their lead. Consciousness has many definitions. Psychologist Nicholas Humphrey, author of A HISTORY OF THE MIND, defines it as "raw sensation", whereas Roger Penrose, a mathematical physicist and author of THE EMPEROR'S NEW MIND, sees consciousness as "the ability to divine or intuit truth from falsity in appropriate circumstances--to form inspired judgements. (1)

The great neurologist Sir John Eccles wrote in EVOLUTION OF THE BRAIN: "Since materialist solutions fail to account for our uniqueness, I am constrained to attribute the uniqueness of the Self or Soul to a supernatural spiritual creation," which, he said, is "a miracle forever beyond science." (2)

I believe consciousness can be studied, but its complexity may never be fully understood if we use only the tools of science. A deeper exploration, into the metaphysical, is probably necessary.

If we understood the laws of physics better the concept of mind would be clearer. Those who study complexity believe there is a set of rules that once identified will unify the life sciences and help us understand complex systems like the human brain.

These laws likely apply to the psychic operation of the human brain as well as its other functions. They will help us comprehend such phenomena as telepathy and psychokinesis, and this will have a great impact on our thinking about ourselves and the physical world.

Before the rise of science causality lacked the influence it has enjoyed in the past two centuries. David Hume, an eighteenth century philosopher, believed a necessary connection between a particular cause and its effect is not a certainty, but a mental habit. (3)

Physicist F. David Peat laments the hold the law of cause and effect has had on the modern world. He considers it an idealization only and not sufficient to understand nature. The whole must be considered in describing phenomena. Small events can contribute to far-reaching consequences. For example, lifting a pool ball on the star Alpha Centuri can disrupt the motion of a gas on earth. (4)

Nature is complex, with a delicate balance between stability and instability. A good illustration is the weather. The fluttering of the wings of a butterfly may start a weather change that will affect an area many miles away.

The whole must be studied in dealing with complex phenomena such as chaos, turbulence, transition, and evolution, where slight effects can be very important. I believe one of these effects is consciousness, and it shows itself in psychokinesis, the use of psychic power to affect the material world. An illustration is the movement of an object by concentrating upon it.

Some believe consciousness has a much larger role in the world. Fred Alan Wolf, in PARALLEL UNIVERSES: THE SEARCH FOR OTHER WORLDS, (5) speculates there would be no objects in the physical world without it. Matter appears to be more fragile than we think. We create our reality, which includes not only the world within ourselves, but the external world as well.

We are uncertain about the nature of reality. Scientists once thought light, essential for life on our planet, was made up of waves, but experiments have shown it has the properties of both waves and particles. Could other particles have wave-like properties? In some studies electrons behaved like light waves, and the observation of atomic particles appeared to alter them.

In others, observers couldn't know a particle's position and momentum at the same time (Heisenberg's uncertainty principle). Douglas R. Hofstadter (6) wrote in METAMAGICAL THEMAS: QUESTING FOR THE ESSENCE OF MIND AND PATTERN: "It's not just that we cannot **know** a particle's position and momentum simultaneously; it doesn't even **have** definite position and momentum simultaneously!"

In the Copenhagen interpretation of quantum mechanics, when a physical system is observed its properties instantly change; its wave form collapses when an observer and the system are connected.

From Seth, Jane Roberts received a somewhat different view of particles, waves, and how they are related to consciousness. In ADVENTURES IN CONSCIOUSNESS she wrote we are particles of energy materialized from the source self, which "...can be thought of as an entity, a personified energy gestalt--energy that knows itself--that creates and then perceives itself through experience, as it constantly sends 'waves' of itself into dimensional activity. These energy waves, striking our system, form the individual 'particle' with its focus (or particle) personality. The energy waves bounce back and forth, to and from the source self, so there is constant interaction." (7)

Numerous "aspect selves", which appear as personality traits, characteristics, and talents, giving us individuality, come from the source self. Our experiences create new energy waves, giving life to fields of energy which lie fallow until our consciousness makes them real in our world.

Reality is created by our brains interpreting frequencies from another dimension, according to the holographic supertheory. In the AQUARIAN CONSPIRACY (8) Marilyn Ferguson compares the brain to a hologram, which encodes information in a picture. With laser light a complete three-dimensional image can be created from even a small portion of the holographic plate, since the entire image is encoded across the whole plate. Ferguson believes our holographic brains interpret an holographic universe.

Psychic phenomena can be explained as a by-product of the holographic matrix. Human brains, as part of the framework, sometimes have access to all the information in the system. Likely the non-verbal right brain is involved. Targ and Puthoff (9) think psi ability may be a function of the right brain. In their remote viewing experiments the participants' general descriptions of the targets were more accurate than their estimates of the size of the objects viewed. Participants often made mistakes in naming objects. Images, which provide global information, are probably picked up by the right brain, whereas language is a left brain function. Remote viewers found reading letters and words difficult. Their drawings were often left-right reversed, perhaps indicating their entire brains were not involved in the experiments.

Psi phenomena are unpredictable and seem capricious because the right brain operates by different rules than the left brain, and when we try to understand right brain functioning with left brain rationality we are lost. Our left brains can neither understand nor control psi. Subtle, like a whisper in the wind, it eludes them.

An example illustrating the mystery of telepathy was my sending a message to a player in a Trivial Pursuit game. The answer to a question was "the Bismarck", which I held in my mind, wondering if she would receive it. She got the impression of a ship but couldn't name it. It seemed her right brain received the image, but the player's verbal left brain couldn't come up with the answer.

Telepathy, or thought transference, likely occurred in both the remote viewing studies and in the Trivial Pursuit game, indicating all brains are connected.

If human consciousness is viewed in the traditional way, as localized within the body, remote viewing and other psychic phenomena (such as telepathy) cannot be explained, in the opinion of physicists Robert Jahn and Brenda Dunne. They wrote MARGINS OF REALITY (10), based on research at Princeton University. The book includes studies of remote viewing and psychokinesis, the latter using polystyrene balls.

Like Jane Roberts, Jahn and Dunne believe consciousness has a wave nature, and it might behave according to wave-mechanical processes. Information is not organized in terms of time and space, but as frequencies and amplitudes of a wave-mechanical system. Human consciousness converts this system to our space/time array. Physical space and time may then be considered ordering parameters. Perhaps consciousness can create information about any segment of space and time.

Quantum mechanical theory challenges conventional views of reality, but it can be used to explain findings in psychic research. Concepts such as wave/particle duality and the role of the observer, "... concede a degree of paradox in human perception of physical processes and suggest that physical theory is less a statement of abstract reality than of our ability to acquire information about that reality." (11)

Jahn and Dunne conclude quantum mechanics has not yet yielded credible hypotheses for psychologists and neurophysiologists to test. It is most useful as a metaphor for conscious interaction.

However, consciousness might have the wave/particle duality proposed for the physical world. If this is so, some psi phenomena, such as remote viewing and precognition, can be explained. In the remote viewing experiments reported by Jahn and Dunne a participant who remained stationary attempted to describe a place to which someone else had been sent by experimenters. The "target" could be as close as the neighborhood or as much as thousands of miles away. Participants showed distance is irrelevant; they were just as likely to accurately describe a place across the country as a location nearby. Time as well appeared to be irrelevant, and there was evidence of precognition when participants correctly described places to which observers would be sent days before they arrived. Was this an example of effect before cause?

If consciousness can take wave form it may be able to leave the body and travel in time and space, making remote viewing possible regardless of where a "target" is or when it will be visited. This seems to be happening in some remote viewing cases where, "... a percipient may report that his consciousness seems to have been totally liberated from its center to roam freely in space and time, which would correspond, in the metaphor, to escape to the free-wave state. In this state consciousness could access remote locations as an outward propagating wave, reflections of which could return information about those locations." (12)   A similar liberation of consciousness has been reported by those who have undergone "near-death" and "out-of-body" experiences.

Phyllis Atwater, (13) a near-death survivor, wrote: "You shift frequencies in dying. You switch over to life on another wavelength. You are still a spot on the (radio) dial but you move up or down a notch or two. You don't die when you die. You shift your consciousness and speed of vibration. That is all death is. A shift."

Atwater experienced the particle nature of consciousness in her "out-of-body" state.   When she started thinking and questioning, dark gray "blobs" began to float in the air around her. "They were blobs, like ink blots, but fully dimensional, buoyant, and without definitive form. The more I thought, the more blobs there were..." (14) They both puzzled and irritated her.

Psychics have long claimed thoughts are things. They also "read vibrations" from people, which reveal personality characteristics, history, and indications of what the future might bring. Predictions of the future can never be totally accurate as the free will of the person in question, as well as others in her life, is involved. The future can be described as possibilities, which Fred Alan Wolf discusses in terms of parallel universes.

"Vibrations", or waves of consciousness, might also affect matter, as in psychokinesis. A person concentrating on an object might be able to move it by means of waves. Resonance of waves between people can explain such mysteries as healing and love at first sight. Resonance might also explain the man/machine anomalies Jahn and Dunne found in psychokinesis experiments. Participants could influence the paths of polystyrene balls, which normally fell at random in a machine.

Different participants, or operators, affected the balls in varying ways. Over many trials small but steady indicators showed operators influenced the balls. Operators had characteristic "signatures". Some changed the paths of balls in the way they intended, but others altered the fall of balls in the opposite direction. The results for some were significantly different from chance only when they manually operated the machine, and for others only when the machine was on automatic. Thus operators had varying relationships with their machine; this might be due to their different waves of consciousness. Most successful operators said their results were due to resonance, or total absorption, where personal awareness was lost. (15)

Jahn and Dunne feel everyone has her own margin of reality, which involves style in processing information and ability to resonate with the environment. Their most fundamental idea is reality is created in the interaction between consciousness and its surroundings.

After my experiences with the mysterious ringing of the smoke detector and my apparent "zapping" of the t.v. I accepted the idea humans create their reality. Although I am among the many who don't understand such scientific topics as quantum mechanics, I appreciate the contributions science has made to man's understanding of nature.

Before the rise of science man made other attempts to comprehend the world. Divination, foretelling the future or finding hidden information through various forms of psychic reading, has been used from ancient times until the present.

"According to the Chinese sages, the act of divination enfolds a moment that contains the essence of the present and the seeds of the future. Divination is therefore the microcosm that reflects the whole of nature and society and includes, within it, the observer." (16)

There are many methods of divination. An ancient Chinese tribe read the cracks in tortoise shells burned with sticks. Later the I Ching came into being. In the west methods such as crystal ball and Tarot card reading have been used for centuries. Astrology and numerology have been practiced for thousands of years by many different cultures.

Numerology, along with other methods of divination, uncovers synchronous patterns. There are nine character traits in numerology, and each letter of the alphabet is assigned a numerical value corresponding to one of them. The letters A, J, and S have the value of 1. Pythagoras interpreted the vibration of sound of these letters and placed them in the 1 category. "The number 1 (A, J, S) represents the creative, changeably progressive loner who is motivated by the ego." (17)

Numbers keep scores in our material world, and they have an unconscious (spiritual) meaning. Jung thought numbers might have been discovered rather than invented. Numbers like 3 have a spiritual significance, as in Christianity's Holy Trinity. We also use them as a way of conceptualizing our world. As my sister Terri said with reference to the birth of three sons to three sisters in our family in twelve months, "Things come in threes."

An illustration of a synchronous pattern that numerology can make sense of is the presidential sequence between 1840 and 1960. (18) Beginning with William H. Harrison's election in 1840 every president elected in a year divisible by 20 died in office. The list includes Lincoln, Garfield, McKinley, Harding, Franklin D. Roosevelt, and Kennedy. Although Ronald Reagan was shot while in office, he survived to complete a second term.

A number of parallels in the assassinations of Lincoln and Kennedy can be understood in terms of numerology. Lincoln was elected president in 1860, and Kennedy was elected in 1960, one hundred years later. Both were killed on Friday, the fifth day of the week. Lincoln was shot in Ford's Theater, and Kennedy was shot in a Lincoln convertible, a product of the Ford Motor Company. The successors of both men were named

Johnson, and were born 100 years apart. The assassins, John Wilkes Booth and Lee Harvey Oswald, both have 15 letters in their names.

Scientists as well as numerologists attempt to understand seemingly related events. Cases like the above lead mathematicians studying coincidence to the conclusion: "The more we work in this area, the more we feel that Kammerer and Jung are right. We are swimming in an ocean of coincidences." (19) Some can be explained in terms of cause and effect or perception, but others have a hidden cause. This might indicate synchronicity.

Astrology, numerology, Tarot, and other methods of divination have had an impact on my life. For years Tarot card readers and psychics told me my book would be a success, and this kept me writing. I believe the practitioners of these arts can read the unconscious minds of their clients by telepathy. The unconscious knows much, including the likelihood of future events.

Numerology is enlightening because it uncovers patterns in our lives which we normally wouldn't notice, helping make sense of synchronous events. Some years ago, when I consulted the INFORMATION PLEASE ALMANAC's (20) perpetual calendar, I discovered patterns in my life. At the time I knew nothing about numerology and guessed the patterns had to do with astrology.

I found years using calendars #2 and #3 have special significance for me, marking cycles. In calendar #2 the year starts and ends on Monday, the day I was born. January 1 and December 31 fall on Tuesday when calendar #3 is used. When calendars #2 and #3 occur a year apart, calendar #2 marks an important beginning in my life, and #3 involves a resolution, or ending. In years where calendars #2 and #3 come six years apart, less significant beginnings and endings, relating to education, occur. All of these events have happened in the warm months--April through September. The following chart shows them.

Calendar	Year	Event
#2	1945 (Aug.)	Conception
#3	1946 (May)	Birth
#2	1951 (Sept.)	Started Elementary School
#3	1957 (Sept.)	Began Last Year Elem. School
#2	1962 (May)	Saw Priest's Aura
#3	1963 (Spring)	Decided to Leave Church
#2	1973 (April)	Met Nat
#3	1974 (May)	Married Nat
#2	1979 (Sept.)	Entered Writers' Class
#3	1985 (Sept.)	Decided to Chair Writers' Gp.
#2	1990 (June)	Found Nat's Father
#3	1991 (July)	Nat's Father Died

Because its practitioners' evaluations of my life are generally true, I believe astrology has some validity. Mark uncovered my fear of having a child and the conflicts my husband and I have over money. I hadn't previously mentioned either of these problems to him.

In addition, an astrologer at a psychic fair told me I have a gift for visualization, and it appears to be true. When I visualize, the desired results occur. I have used the gift mainly to heal, and the health of everyone visualized well has improved.

To satisfy my curiosity about astrology I worked on my horoscope, with the help of Joseph Goodavage's WRITE YOUR OWN HOROSCOPE (21) and ASTRO BASICS ONE. (22) Marlene recommended Goodavage, and she suggested I order a basic horoscope from Astro Communications, to get the positions of the planets at my birth.

Several themes emerged, among them independence and leadership. The moon in Aries and Scorpio ascending suggest resourcefulness and self-reliance as well as leadership ability. Mars in Leo and the moon in Aries predict success in a position of authority. Gemini, my sun sign, supports Scorpio in forecasting ambition.

My chart shows an interest in psi. Venus and Saturn in Cancer point to psychic research, and Neptune in Libra a fascination with magic and the mystical. The moon in Aries also signifies an attraction to mysticism. Uranus in Gemini forecasts talent in e.s.p.

Favorable social traits are shown with Mercury in Gemini (generosity, good humor, and a lack of bias), Venus in Cancer (loyalty, and a loving, sympathetic nature), Mars in Leo (friendliness and a keen sense of justice), and Jupiter and Neptune in Libra (compassion and a love of peace).

Mars in Leo discloses an ardent, passionate side, with a tendency to rush into romance. Scorpio ascending and Venus in Cancer warn of secret affairs and more than one marriage.

Love of learning is another theme. Jupiter in Libra reveals a love of intellectual stimulation, and Uranus in Gemini enjoyment of study and scientific thinking, and ability in languages. The sun in Gemini indicates delight in experimentation, and teaching ability. Mercury in Gemini supports talent in languages and teaching. Neptune in Libra shows an admiration of science.

Mars in Leo predicts creative energy, and Scorpio ascending a fertile imagination. Neptune in Libra and the sun in Gemini also signify a good imagination.

Finally, travel is denoted by Jupiter in Libra. Scorpio ascending may mean business trips to foreign countries.

Studying my horoscope excited and fascinated me, and I learned about myself and my relationships. With Scorpio as my ascendant sign I have "a core of incredible strength, great willpower and endurance". (23) On many occasions I have considered myself weak, but I realized this isn't generally true when I read the ASTRO BASICS report.

With Saturn in Cancer (my husband's sun sign), I was likely to marry an older, serious man who would stimulate me to operate an economical household, and I did. The horoscope helped me to appreciate our relationship. My frugality seemed overshadowed by his, but making good use of resources has always been a priority for me.

Saturn in Cancer also indicates a problem in home life, perhaps because of children. Our son is hyperactive, and since I am sensitive, as Saturn in Cancer predicts, I suffer greatly from the discord his behavior brings.

Generally, the horoscope is an accurate reflection of my life. ASTRO BASICS advises its readers to pay attention to repeated issues and characteristics. I did, and feel this reduced the inevitable bias in analyzing one's own attributes. There were several indicators for leadership and teaching ability, an interest in both science and psi, an active imagination, as well as compassion and a love of peace. I have all these traits. Correspondence between the chart and my life is absent only in facility with languages and number of marriages. I have failed to master a foreign language, which disappoints me. Part of the problem stems from Attention Deficit Disorder; many affected people have problems with language. My horoscope helps explain my mental "affair" with Mohari, but it predicts more than one marriage. So far I have only been married once.

Despite the faith a lot of people have in astrology, many grant it little respect. One reason is astrology has stagnated, some say since the time of the ancient Greeks. Many astrologers cast horoscopes without concern for how and why astrology works. This doesn't help anyone to understand the art, or improve it, which would lead to greater respectability. Another problem is the uncritical acceptance of astrological readings, including daily horoscopes in newspapers. This provides no incentive for astrology's development.

These attitudes were in part responsible for an "official" attack on astrology, when 186 prominent scientists condemned it as fraud and declared it dangerous to society. THE HUMANIST magazine published "Objections to Astrology" in September of 1975. (24) The declaration, signed by astrophysicists and other scientists, cautioned the public against accepting the advice and predictions of astrologers. It stated in part: "Those who wish to believe astrology should realize that there is no scientific foundation for its tenets...It is simply a mistake to imagine that the forces exerted by stars and planets at the moment of birth can in any way shape our futures..."

Unfortunately the public hasn't been well informed about the circumstances of the attack. Two investigators showed nearly all the scientists signing the statement against astrology had done no research on the subject. No studies in sociology were given to illustrate astrology's negative impact on society. Research later undertaken by some of the scientists actually supported planetary influences, but the media attempted to suppress these results.

The attack on astrology is partially due to a misunderstanding. The widely held belief that the position of the planets at birth **causes** a person to have certain traits is false. Birth under the sun sign of Taurus does not **cause** a woman to become furious when provoked. More knowledgeable astrologers know the planets neither cause character traits nor behavior. The position of the planets merely predicts them.

Psychologist Michel Gauquelin attempted a scientific study of astrology. After he tried to disprove it by statistics, his data surprized him by showing the position of some planets at birth correlates with a person's eventual career choice, and sometimes his success in it.

The results of his study of the birth charts of 576 medical doctors showed they had a tendency to be born immediately after Mars or Saturn had risen or come to the highest point in its daily journey in the sky. Other people didn't exhibit this tendency. Gauquelin thought his findings absurd, and he was embarrassed. He repeated his study with 508 additional eminent doctors and obtained the same results. (25)

By investigating thousands of people in various occupations living in a number of countries Michel Gauquelin and his wife Francoise discovered a pattern. The more successful a group was in a field, the more they tended to have a related planet in certain places of their birth charts. Gauquelin named these areas of the sky "key sectors" and considered them more accurate for astrological readings than the traditional houses.

Mars is often in a key sector when great doctors, athletes, or soldiers are born, but it avoids key sectors when artists, painters, and musicians come into the world. Ministers, politicians, and writers often have the moon in key sectors, while athletes and soldiers do not.

The Gauquelins used statistics to study the relationship between time of birth and certain personality characteristics, in addition to occupational data. When Mars is in a "plus zone" (key sector) at a person's birth she will likely be brave, energetic, and strong-willed. Those born with the moon in a "plus zone" tend to be disorganized, friendly, and imaginative. Both groups show spontaneity.

Unlike traditional astrology, the Gauquelins' neo-astrology considers only five planets important in birth charts: Jupiter, Saturn, Mars, Venus, and the Moon (considered a planet for astrological purposes). They haven't been able to find any evidence for a connection between a person's character and the position of the sun, Mercury, Uranus, Neptune and Pluto at his birth.

Gauquelin's use of statistics departs from the approach of traditional astrologers, many of whom believe the universe is ruled by synchronicity. An example of synchronicity is former classmates, who haven't seen one another in years, "accidentally" meeting exactly ten years after they graduated.

To a believer in synchronicity everything that exists is connected with everything else, and a pattern among the planets may reflect another pattern, such as a woman's personality. The position of the planets at a man's birth reflects his character because of interrelatedness--the planets do not **cause** him to become a brave soldier or a disorganized dreamer. The individual born when Mars is rising has certain inclinations, but he can choose to be a physician, athlete, soldier, or anything else, although he might be more successful in the above occupations than in other fields.

Gauquelin didn't believe the positions of the planets **cause** a person's character. He thought the fetus has a "planetary sensibility" which stimulates its birth at a given time. Planets themselves don't affect the personalities of individuals, but only act as "triggers" for birth. The position of planets at birth **reflects** temperament; it does not **cause** it.

Gauquelin's planetary sensibility supports synchronicity. It strengthens the theory by providing a mechanism for its operation. When a girl is born under a certain sky it is as if she is saying, "This is the kind of person I am." If born at the time the moon is rising she may be telling the world, "I will be a tolerant, but impulsive woman likely to be successful in politics or writing."

Percy Seymour, principal lecturer in astronomy at the Plymouth Polytechnic Institute in England, has refined the idea of planetary sensibility. (26) He believes the behavior of the fetus at birth is linked to cycles in the Earth's geomagnetic field, which is influenced by the solar cycle and planet positions. The fetus resonates with these cycles. His nervous system acts as an antenna, picking up fluctuations of the Earth's field which synchronize the fetus' biological clock, controlling his birth time.

The tuning of the antenna is genetic, and Seymour believes to some extent it determines inherited personality characteristics. The position of the planets at birth doesn't alter inheritance, but it **labels** inherited personality characteristics.

Seymour's ideas on heredity might be better understood by referring to Gauquelin's finding on the similarities of the skies at birth between parents and their children, indicating planetary heredity. (27) If a child's father or mother is born with a planet in one of the "plus zones" the child tends to be born with the same planet in the same zone, indicating similar heredity with regard to personality traits.

Gauquelin was disappointed because in 1984 he couldn't reproduce the results of his earlier studies showing planetary heredity, but this may due to induced births and Caesarean sections, which have increased dramatically in recent years. In these births it is the doctor and not the child who decides when an infant will come into the world. With surgical intervention planetary heredity disappears.

The work of Gauquelin and Seymour shows how two approaches, one scientific and one ancient and based on synchronicity, can be successfully blended. I consider this a harbinger of the future, when scientists explain the paranormal. Then the practitioners of astrology, numerology and other methods of divination will receive greater respect, and society will benefit from their wisdom.

Chapter Eight

Colin And Other Miracles

In 1983 I returned to the concrete world, and I seldom thought of "checking out" again. Pregnancy, and the events surrounding it, led to a greater involvement with others and their problems. Although still tuned in to the psychic world, I focused most on the people and things surrounding me.

My dreams the previous year reflected the change. Just before Halloween of 1982 came one of bearing a baby boy. Later I dreamed Nat and I went to New Orleans. A road outside the city was blocked for crop irrigation. When we stopped the sugar cane plantation owner asked me to take care of his puppy for ten days, while he traveled. I had to refuse because my blonde, curly-haired little girl needed me at home.

The dream was meaningful because I had been trying to conceive for seven years. Two of my sisters were pregnant; one was due in days. Happy for them, but sorry for myself, I spent a lot of time pouting, wishing I were having a baby.

I wondered what was wrong with me. Doctors could find no reason we had been unable to conceive, and with sorrow I had nearly given up on having a family. Nat wouldn't permit fertility drugs, and he refused to adopt a child.

Still I had hopes and dreams. One day I saw a birth sampler in the craft section of a store near my house. It was unusual, with a mother and infant worked in brown floss. With every trip to the store I looked at it, imagining the beautiful baby were mine. At home I thought of that child, and I anticipated returning to the store to see it.

It happened in March. Frequent trips to the bathroom were the first sign. After that the nausea and fatigue began. Betty delivered her first child, a son, at the end of the month. Terri's little boy had been born the previous November. Was it my turn? I was optimistic, but cautious. If too much excitement caused a miscarriage I would be devastated. Still, I could hardly wait to buy the embroidery kit.

In April a pregnancy test confirmed what I had suspected. My sister Sandy drove me to the clinic. I asked her to go in with me, but she preferred to wait for the results in her car. "Guess what?" I beamed as I rejoined her. "I'm pregnant." Sandy remained silent as she started the engine.

I tried to understand her feelings. Our other two married sisters had baby boys, and Loren's two daughters brightened family gatherings. Of the women in our family only Sandy and Renee, who is mentally ill, remained childless. In addition, the principal at Sandy's school was pressuring the teachers to achieve more with their students. He forced one of Sandy's friends to repeat her student teaching; she had taught for twenty years.

When I told Nat we were going to have a baby he wasn't happy either. He said we couldn't afford a child. At the time he worked as a contract employee at General Motors, and the future seemed uncertain.

The week after my pregnancy test Sandy became more depressed. She gave up her apartment, storing her furniture at the homes of relatives, including ours. A conscientious teacher, Sandy decided not to finish the school year and divided her time between our house and Mom's until fall. By then she felt well enough to return to school, but she continued to live with Mom.

Renee didn't fare as well. By fall she had been admitted to a state hospital. When Nat and I visited her we discovered a confusing place. We tried to find the proper entrance three times before we succeeded. Then we went through a maze before finding the lobby. When we got to Renee's floor three doors bore the same name.

I knocked on one door, and a woman came out of another behind me. Her piercing gaze frightened me. When I at last found the correct door to the waiting room, a visitor looked at me with suspicion. Only the employees in the lobby treated me as a sane person. I wondered how anyone got well there, but Renee improved, leaving the hospital for a group home in a few months.

Nat's attitude improved as the pregnancy progressed, but acceptance took a long time. When anyone asked him if he wanted a boy or a girl, he replied, "a puppy." He changed his mind when we found from amniocentesis the child was a boy. Then he envisioned camping trips to national parks with his soon-to-be companion.

Two aunts lost their husbands during my pregnancy. One was Uncle Bob. Years before I had visualized his arm healing. It had improved, but shortly before his death his diagnosis was Alzheimer's Disease, which he had probably suffered for a long time.

In addition to keeping up with my family, I prepared for the baby. I read a lot about pregnancy and childbirth, exercised, made maternity clothes, attended Lamaze classes, and decorated the nursery. Shopping for baby clothes and equipment, and keeping doctor appointments filled out my schedule.

Nurses found it difficult to measure our son's heart rate in the last months because he moved frequently. He often kicked me, and sometimes it hurt. I was carrying an active baby, and I worried he might be hyperactive. If so he would be a challenge to raise.

From my pregnancy to the present I have had little time or energy for the psychic world. Although I still think of Mohari, wondering who he is and why he came to transform my life, the obsession has never returned.

My psychic involvement abated before Colin's birth, but my awareness of phenomena such as presences, synchronicity, and the power of visualization continue. The difference is they no longer rule me.

My pregnancy was normal, and the baby seemed healthy. Labor lasted a little over twelve hours, but what Mark had predicted proved true. There was some trouble. When Dr. La

France broke my water it appeared greenish, indicating fetal distress, and he set up a fetal monitor. The delivery went badly-- I pushed for two hours without success. Finally Dr. La France delivered Colin by caesarean section.

During surgery I thought of the mothers throughout time who hadn't survived childbirth, and I grieved for them. I told the anesthesiologist, who had an east Indian accent, if I were in a poor country this would probably be the end for me. He told me not to think about it, but thoughts of the deaths of mothers during childbirth and the sorrow it caused persisted for months. I may have been tuning into an energy field, perhaps a morphogenetic field, (1) where the memories of those who died in childbirth reside. Perhaps my connection with the field is strong because my great-great grandmother died shortly after giving birth to my great grandmother, and her family split as a result.

Undergoing the C-section I hadn't realized my closeness to death. Later my husband confided Dr. La France had been worried as my pushing had damaged vessels, and I lost a lot of blood. Fortunately my obstetrician thought I would survive without a blood transfusion. In 1983 the procedure was risky, because of HIV infected blood.

I **knew** I would be all right. At the beginning of my pregnancy the feeling I would need a C-section had concerned me, but in 1983 they were relatively safe.

When I saw Colin the ordeal lost its importance. He had brown hair, big dark eyes, and his skin was ivory. I had hoped it would be darker, like his father's, so he wouldn't burn in the sun, but his skin was beautiful. Before we left the hospital he smiled, and I felt proud.

The day after discharge I returned; because of intestinal blockage I couldn't urinate. Waiting in the emergency room for two hours, I thought my bladder would burst and did Lamaze breathing to cope with the pain. A nurse drained my bladder, and I was admitted to the hospital. I felt snatched from death for the second time that week. Someone or something protected me. Was it Mohari?

After I returned home and was well enough to work on the birth sampler my mother remarked, "Colin looks just like that baby." I agreed. With his brown hair and eyes, and similar facial features, Colin resembled the sampler child. Sandy suggested I work the mother to look like me, with auburn hair and green eyes, and I did. I thought about Jane Roberts' belief we create our own reality. Had my concentration on the birth sampler made me more active in Colin's creation than most parents, or was I just more aware of my contribution?

The fact my sisters and I had sons within a year is an example of synchronicity. The many cases in which sisters and close friends are pregnant at the same time illustrates the linkage of women. We may be able to trigger one another's hormones, which leads to ovulation. Then we can share the joys and stress of motherhood together, supporting each other.

Terri recognized the connection. Before I knew of my pregnancy, she said, "Things come in threes." She expressed disappointment when I told her I wouldn't have a second child, in part because of my age. "The girls are coming," she told me. Both Terri's and Betty's second-born children are girls. Terri's has blond curls, like the child in my dream of New Orleans.

Of the five children born to my sisters and me, Colin seems most vulnerable. In infancy he had colic, screaming and vomiting every evening. He spoke few words at the age of three, when I took him to a speech therapist. He was a fussy eater, refusing meat, poultry, eggs, and fish. Toilet training wasn't complete until he attended Kindergarten.

As a hyperactive child he got into a lot of trouble. Before he was two he hit his head on the edge of the coffee table and required internal and external stitches. He also fell on the hearth of the fireplace, which left part of his lip hanging from his mouth, tumbled downstairs in his walker, and ate mushrooms from the back yard. All of these accidents required visits to the emergency room--Nat and I were glad we carried extra medical insurance. Any one of these incidents could have been disastrous, but Colin has only slight scars to remind us of his early mishaps. I often think someone is watching over him.

I was convinced of the intervention of a higher power when Colin developed pneumonia at the age of five. During the winter of 1989, Colin coughed every night when he went to bed and resumed hacking in the morning. When his coughing increased on a Sunday in February, we took him to a drop-in clinic, where the physician recommended a non-prescription cold medicine. This angered me as I had given Colin a similar over-the-counter medication, which hadn't helped.

Keeping him out of school, I nursed Colin, but after two days his persistent cough worried me. I returned to the clinic. A different doctor gave us a prescription, but it was too late.

The next day Colin coughed constantly. I called the clinic twice, but the receptionist didn't recommend an office visit. When his coughs came seventy seconds apart we went to the office.

The doctor said she suspected pneumonia and took Colin for x-rays. I broke down. "I tried. I tried." I sobbed.

In a few minutes the x-ray results terrified me--the doctor had found a spot on Colin's lung, and she recommended hospitalization. Still crying, I left the office with Colin as quickly as I could.

I was angry with myself as well as the clinic. I should have taken Colin to Dr. Hawthorne on Monday. Arriving home I called our family doctor and drove Colin to the hospital as soon as I could pack his belongings. A favorite blanket and his stuffed rabbit accompanied us. Colin had eaten and drunk little during his illness and was dehydrated. Nurses had trouble attaching an i.v. He coughed constantly. I thought we would lose him that night.

I have a strong faith in my psychic ability, especially in visualization. I stayed in Colin's room all night, determined to save him. Using all the strength I could garner, I concentrated on Colin, picturing him well. I had little time for sleep that first night at the hospital. When I didn't imagine white light around Colin, or pray for him, I ran for a nurse to reconnect the i.v., which Colin disconnected when he coughed. Then at 5:00 a.m. came the break. Our son stopped coughing, and I knew he would live. Tears filled my eyes as I thanked God and sent Colin more light. Then I fell asleep.

Later that morning Dr. Hawthorne made his rounds. "Colin must be an awfully strong little boy," he remarked. "There is only one spot on his lung."

Prayer and visualization unleash powerful forces. I prayed and visualized Sandy finding a teaching position in another school, and she did. When she received the news she asked if it were my doing. I smiled and told her, "Maybe."

Calling upon the power within me, and beyond, also helped me move from the south, and ultimately into my dream house. Before Colin's birth I had sketched the floor plan of the house I wanted, which we would build if necessary. The three bedroom brick ranch with two baths would sit on a large lot with trees.

The house was not extraordinary, but large wooded lots were uncommon in our area. After Colin came our remodeled home, with the master bedroom a floor away from the nursery, no longer met our needs. We decided to move, and we looked at houses for months. I had given up on my dream home, and Nat and I nearly purchased a brick ranch with only one tree in the yard.

Then I did something unusual--I bought a suburban newspaper. On one of its pages a large ranch with a yard full of trees enticed me. Although our real estate agent was unfamiliar with the neighborhood, she showed us the property. It had all we wanted, including a 2 1/2 car garage where Nat could easily store the lawn mower, yard tools, bicycles, outdoor furniture in winter, and still park both cars.

When I first saw the carpeting in the family room the coincidence amazed me--it matched the orange shag of our family room in the south. The same mirror tile hung on the dining room wall as in the family room of our second house. A charming courtyard with an iron gate graced the entrance, and peach and pink roses, my favorite flowers, decorated it. In the back yard raspberry bushes grew, reminding me of my childhood. Nat loves raspberries. It was as if the house, built the year of our marriage, had been created for us. On our first visit we altered and signed the contract originally meant for the house with one tree. Later we discovered the first name of our home's former owner is Colin, and a Colin family lives next door, illustrating more synchronicity.

I felt at ease in my new home. Mysterious night music and "presences" were absent. The year before we moved out of our two-story home the weekend music had become louder. I had heard a man's voice talking over it more than once, which frightened me. When I went into the yard to check if the sounds were coming from the outside, the silence puzzled me. I heard the music again when I returned to the house.

Secure in the ranch, I felt free to pursue my interests. In early 1985, after we were settled, I joined the local newcomers' club and discovered a writers' group. The later included only a handful of members, and sometimes so few attended the leader considered disbanding it. After I had gone for a year she announced her husband was retiring, and they would travel the country in their camper. Denise and I volunteered to take over the group, but when my friend returned to college she was too busy to help me. I placed announcements in local newspapers and recruited new members on my own.

Cliff, an author of romance novels, came to the first meeting I chaired. He suffered from heart disease, and his doctors recommended a coronary bypass. He had refused to undergo the surgery as he wasn't sure it would solve his problem in the long run.

Cliff wanted to break out of the romance genre and had started a Viking novel. He asked if I would edit it. The work would be time-consuming, but manageable as I no longer taught psychology classes. Cliff was told I would have to schedule the editing around Colin, a very active toddler who didn't sleep as many hours as most children his age.

I worked with Cliff for a year, and the results pleased us. The well-researched manuscript featured vivid images and a gentle tone. Action scenes swept the story along, although the overall pace was slower. Cliff reluctantly reduced the violence in the Viking attacks. I told him it was not in keeping with the tone of the book for the Vikings to rape and slaughter nuns and decapitate a priest during mass. Although this might have happened, the reader wouldn't sympathize with characters who performed such atrocities.

In contrast, Cliff had no problem creating a likable heroine, daughter of the Viking leader. The mother of the out-of-wedlock child had died in childbirth. Nuns raised the beautiful, sweet-tempered girl. Her father found Elanor when he attacked the religious community where she lived.

I hadn't been able to edit the book rapidly enough for Cliff, so we weren't on good terms when I finished. Long before he had stopped attending writers' group meetings because he did not wish to read portions of his novel. Members considered Cliff a gifted writer and couldn't understand his reluctance to share his story with them.

Working with Cliff gave me confidence in my writing and editing ability. When Colin started preschool I began using my free time to record my experiences with reincarnation and psi. First I wrote an autobiography, but it lacked focus on the metaphysical. With the help of writers' groups and conferences the manuscript took form, and the shadows--Mohari, the "presences", dreams, e.s.p., and my past lives--synthesized in SHADOWS ON MY MIND.

Inspiration was Cliff's gift to me, and although his irritability had driven me away, I wished him well. I wasn't prepared for the phone call on a hot August afternoon. Two years after I had last spoken with Cliff, Danielle, a writer friend, phoned with the shocking news he was dead. Cliff had apparently shot himself.

An elderly mutual friend had spoken to him shortly before his death. Disturbed at the tragic news, the former writers' group member called me. She confided Cliff had been angry because his agent hadn't been able to place the Viking novel. She didn't know he had been contemplating suicide.

Strange events occurred after Cliff's death. Grieving for him the night after he died, I went to the bedroom and turned on Channel 7's 11:00 news. Still in shock, I collapsed on the bed. As soon as my head touched the pillow a cricket outside the window began screaming so loud it drowned the program. I turned up the volume. Although I could hear the commentators, the shrill sound unnerved me. I switched on the room air conditioner, but the chirping was still audible.

Was Cliff telling me he had survived death? He had been uncertain of an afterlife but listened with an open mind when I explained reincarnation and other beliefs. I warned him against suicide as Marlene had told me those who die by their own hand can't communicate with other spirits. By some accounts they agonize alone in a dark world.

Because I thought Cliff would die before me, and guiding him to the other side wouldn't be possible, I had instructed him to go to the light. Before he left the earth plane he could visit me. "Just don't come through the walls," I reminded him. "I couldn't handle it. Knock on the door during the day."

An angry man, Cliff had verbally abused me at times. Would he honor my wish to appear only in daylight? I couldn't be certain, and I feared he would show himself at any moment. My body tensed as I listened to the cricket, hoping it (he) would stay outside. Head throbbing, I went to the kitchen for aspirin. Maybe when I left the room the cricket would go too.

When I returned to the bedroom the cricket was still chirping. It disturbed me, but at least it was outside the bedroom window.

By this time I had told Nat I thought Cliff had taken the form of a cricket. Carlos Castaneda (2) wrote of spirits inhabiting animal bodies. Don Juan had assumed a crow's form, and Castaneda had mentioned a cricket as a possibility for embodiment.

I had informed Cliff spirits could take over the bodies of animals as well as humans. I shared with him the story of a man entering an owl during and out-of-body experience. Owls aren't conscious like humans, and the man found its life empty. Nevertheless, Cliff remarked he would like to be a bird.

Nat didn't believe a spirit could assume the form of an animal, but he had no explanation for the chirping. As always, he tolerated my beliefs. He tried to calm me by drawing my mind away from the cricket, talking about the news of the day.

My husband and I didn't get much sleep for two nights after Cliff died. On the second night the cricket awakened Nat at 4:00

a.m., and he couldn't get back to sleep. I slept fitfully, awakening a number of times both nights, afraid Cliff was watching us, wondering if he had the power to show himself.

Nat and I tried to ignore the chirping, but on the second night I decided to stop the aggravation. We were both miserable from lack of sleep. It might help if I acknowledged Cliff's presence.

On the morning of the third day I went outdoors and stood beside the bedroom window. I told Cliff of my sorrow about his "demise" but asked him to stop disturbing our sleep and go to the light. "There is no Hell," I assured him.

That night the chirps weren't as loud; they sounded like those of a normal cricket. I was relieved. The next evening they blended with the other sounds of darkness. The loud chirping had ceased.

Knowing Cliff, I wasn't convinced he had left Earth. I occasionally felt a presence, and one night, as I lay in bed thinking of him, my bedside lamp came on. The old lamp has a weak switch. I've had trouble turning it on, but it had never before switched on by itself.

Months after Cliff's death came a rare experience: I saw a dark eagle on a utility pole next to a well-traveled suburban road. I was driving Colin to school that morning, and it frightened me. I imagined it attacking the car, although that was unlikely. I thought of Cliff. Was he trying to tell me he was still earth-bound? He once said he would like to be a bird, and he identified with eagles. One was tattooed on his upper arm, and he used the birds as decorations in his home. Cliff owned Indian artifacts and enjoyed reading about Native Americans. For a long time I had suspected one of his incarnations had been responsible for the death of White Cloud, and we had met to settle a karmic score, only partially rectified when Grandpa killed the hawk.

I suspected the same involvement in the Indian life with my father-in-law, who also liked eagles. If the story is true he and Cliff may have been embodied as the Indians who tied White Cloud near the eagles' nest. Dad died a month before Cliff. Although she didn't care for it, Erena, Dad's second wife, had bought him an expensive ceramic eagle. He treasured his Christmas gift. Dad had named a favorite eagle at the National

Zoo, and he visited it frequently. Shortly before he died I purchased him a book on eagles as a Father's Day gift, which he appreciated.

I hadn't known Dad for long. He and Nat's mother had divorced in the 1950's, and Nat and his brother hadn't seen their father in 32 years when we found him in 1990. We had tried to make contact with him for several years before we succeeded.

It seemed we were meant to find him; a synchronous chain of events led us to him. While cleaning her Minnesota house the summer before she sold it, Nat's mother found an old trunk. In the bottom she discovered an 1884 history book, where Nat's ancestors were listed among the first settlers of Fort Randolf, Virginia. Nat's family knew his father had grown up in Virginia, and in the 1960's Nat and his mother had tried to locate Dad's ancestral home, but his mother had forgotten the name of the town.

Nat and I had planned to vacation in Virginia the following summer. We decided to explore Fort Randolf after visiting my sister Terri and her family. Maybe someone there would know the whereabouts of Nat's father.

When Nat shared his plan with a coworker who had family in Virginia, she recommended he find a church in the town. Nat contacted the minister of the only church, and he said we could visit him.

On June seventh we left Michigan. The first day of travel proved routine, but the next day we knew this would be an extraordinary trip. After stopping at a Pennsylvania restaurant around noon, our Chevy's engine died. Six-year-old Colin began walking with his dad to a nearby gas station while I remained with the car. When an orange hatchback pulled up and Nat talked to the occupants for several minutes, I was surprised. We didn't know anyone in that vicinity. Then the car halted behind me, and I recognized a woman Nat had taught with at a Pennsylvania college eighteen years before. She and her husband still lived near the college, 150 miles from our breakdown. They were on their way to visit their son in Washington D.C.

After the car had been repaired and we had visited Terri, we drove to Fort Randolf, a village of two streets. We dropped by the home of the town minister, and followed his car to the two homes Nat's family had owned. Later he directed us to the cemetery.

The afternoon was hot and humid, and after a few minutes of searching for family graves I was ready to leave. Then a pink floral arrangement drew my eye. I moved it aside, as it covered the name on the tombstone. What I saw made me tremble. The stone read: Leona Victoria Gates.

Nat's Grandmother! She had died in 1968, after many years of illness. Why the expensive flowers? Unless ... Nat's father had returned to Virginia. Hoping to find him, I grabbed a piece of paper and began writing a note to leave with the flowers.

Then a car drove up behind us. A middle-aged woman in a white blouse and dark skirt emerged, and Nat told her we were tracing his family. Mrs. Moore said she had known some of them, including Aunt Barbara, whom Nat hadn't heard from since childhood. After she watered the flowers on her husband's grave she promised to look for Aunt Barbara's address. Mrs. Moore had intended to water them the day before, but she had returned late from a trip. We were grateful she had waited until we arrived at the cemetery.

Mrs. Moore took us to her well-maintained home, located cards and letters, and began looking through them at her dining room table. As she shuffled through stacks of mail we became more excited by the minute. Time dragged as we paced the large living room. We assured Mrs. Moore if she couldn't find the address that night we would phone her later. Then she found her 1989 Christmas cards. Aunt Barbara's was among them, complete with her address. Nat and I rejoiced, thanking Mrs. Moore again and again.

"We're going to find him at last," I told my husband as we drove back to the motel.

Friday morning Nat called his aunt, and she gave him his father's phone number, with a warning her brother had cancer. Shocked, we knew we had to contact him immediately, before it was too late. We were eager to meet him, but his illness robbed us of some of the joy.

When Nat called his father cried, "Erena, it's Nat!" He said he normally left the house early in the morning, but he had a doctor appointment later that day and decided to stay home. He asked us to visit that afternoon.

A slender man, slightly stooped, waited at the entrance of the Arlington condominium. He opened the door to the spacious lobby, where we met Erena. Her smile at our son revealed deep dimples. Nat turned to his father, his hand on the boy's shoulder, "We named him Colin, after you."

We spent a wonderful Father's Day weekend with Dad and Erena, whom he had met as an army officer in Germany. Saturday Dad showed us his favorite exhibits at the National Zoo, including the eagles, while Erena prepared a delicious German dinner, featuring wienerschnitzel. At dinner Dad discussed his illness, cancer of the pancreas. Three years before doctors had revealed he had only a month to live. He credited exercises and Erena's cooking for his survival.

On Father's Day Erena served a lovely champagne brunch. I most enjoyed the blintzes with blueberries. Afterward we presented Dad with the parrot mug we had purchased at the zoo. Dad appreciated the birds of red, green and yellow. Erena gave us a portrait of Dad and herself before we left. Taken on a cruise, it showed Erena in a black satin dress and Dad in a suit. They made a handsome couple.

Dad never told us why he hadn't answered Nat's letters, which the army had forwarded. Erena said they had decided against it when Nat mentioned we would leave the south. It hurt. I didn't understand why Michigan was too far away for them to respond to our letters.

We had to initiate contact by finding them. They treated us well, however, so we didn't spoil the relationship by venting our anger over past wrongs. We wanted to get to know Dad in the time he had left. It meant a lot to all of us.

I believe we found Nat's father because we all had a strong desire to meet. Dad's cancer would take his life, and he knew it.

He wanted to make amends with us before he died, and he delayed his death four years to accomplish this.

Maggie Callanan and Patricia Kelley, nurses who care for the dying, believe: "Some dying people realize they will die more peacefully under certain conditions; until those conditions are met, they may delay the timing of their deaths. This differs from knowing when they will die; some people **do** know and **do** indicate when death will happen, others actually choose the moment of death." (3)

All of us are part of a mind network, and people both inside and outside the family helped bring us together because of the messages we sent, both conscious and unconscious. Synchronicity provided evidence for the network, and irony showed itself, not uncommon in cases like this. We might have found Nat's father buried in the graveyard; instead we met someone who helped us find him alive. The whole process of discovery gave me a greater appreciation for the workings of the universe.

Two nights before Dad passed away, in July of 1991, I dreamed he was dying. He asked us to visit him, and I promised to send Nat. The next day I told him about the dream as we left to camp on Mackinaw Island, but Nat didn't want to cancel our trip. When we returned four days afterward it was too late. Dad had died. His wife said it wasn't an easy death. Perhaps he would have died more peacefully if we had been present.

For months after his death Dad contacted me, asking for forgiveness and prayers. I have prayed for him, and tried to understand why he chose to ignore Nat and his brother for years, but anger remains.

I consider both Cliff and my father-in-law difficult men. Finding it hard to compromise, they needed to have their own way. Cliff harbored a lot of anger within, and I suspect Dad did as well. Both of them loved the symbol of our country, who lives by attacking and killing other animals. I had an unreasonable fear of eagles, in part because I find their behavior distasteful.

Had Amanda feared eagles? If we are facets of the entity of which White Cloud is part, she should have harbored negative feelings toward them. In order to shed light on this and other concerns I decided to contact Amanda's daughter.

Chapter Nine

The Two Amandas And Me

In April of 1992, after working on SHADOWS ON MY MIND for over four years, I called Amanda Jones. I hadn't spoken to her in twelve years because I didn't want to affect future research on her mother. Plagued by uncertainty, it took me a long time to decide how to study my past life. In the interim I had been writing about my psychic experiences, and reading books on physics, psi, and reincarnation. Until I read Dr. Stevenson's books on past life research I wasn't sure Amanda had been a previous personality of mine.

Psychiatrist Ian Stevenson, the world's best-known reincarnation investigator, found one of the most common past-life recollections is the death scene. From reading his work, I suspected the story of Anna and Mohari was a fantasy, and the only true recollection of my last past life was Amanda's death.

Perhaps I could find support Amanda was my predecessor by speaking with her daughter. Dr. Stevenson believes certain aspects of personality are passed on from one life to the next. In CHILDREN WHO REMEMBER PREVIOUS LIVES (1) he indicated the persistence of behavior traits in general is important in the study of past and current lives. Of special interest is the inflexibility of attitudes. I decided to ask Mrs. Jones about her mother's attitudes, aspirations, beliefs, and values, as well as her behavior. I had written Dr. Stevenson for suggestions on the questions to ask, but he could offer no guidelines. He has little faith in inventories and questionnaires family members have filled out on the personalities involved in his studies. One reason is present and previous families often know each other when the inventories are completed.

Despite Dr. Stevenson's opinion I decided to question Mrs. Jones about her mother. I could think of no other way to uncover personal information on Amanda. It took two weeks to prepare a ten-page questionnaire, covering everything from Amanda's appearance and how she decorated her home to her job history, interests, attitudes and values. When it was completed I called Mrs. Jones.

Her reaction to my call was matter-of-fact; she seemed as open-minded about reincarnation as in my last conversation with her years before. Mrs. Jones promised to do her best on the questionnaire. She would also send pictures of her mother, which excited me.

For a month I eagerly awaited her response. At first I was patient, as Mr. Jones had recently passed away. Then I wondered if the questionnaire and pictures had been lost in the mail. When I called Mrs. Jones she confessed grieving over her husband's death had delayed her. Another problem was the younger Amanda hadn't known her parents well. Her parents' generation had considered sharing feelings, especially negative ones, a sign of weakness. Mrs. Jones couldn't answer the detailed questionnaire because of this, and faded memories of what had occurred over forty years before. Instead she had sent a brief letter about her mother with the pictures.

The envelope came on my birthday--the best gift I could have received. I was pleased with the snapshots of a middle-aged Amanda, which reveal a lot about her. She was 5' 7" tall, I later found out from her daughter. I am 5'6 1/2" tall. From the neck down we resemble one another, with our broad shoulders, small breasts, large hands, and shapely legs. In one picture Amanda wore a jacket and skirt set resembling one I had owned several years ago. I still favor jacket and skirt outfits.

Unlike mine, her hair was dark. Later Mrs. Jones said her mother's hair was jet black, unusual for a person of Danish descent. She had very blue eyes, but she tanned well. My eyes are green, and I have auburn hair and light skin, which burns easily. I would love a good tan, but I never have been able to get one.

Jenny Cockell (2) also looked for past-life differences in appearance. Mary, her previous personality, wore her long hair in a bun, and as a child Jenny didn't like her curly hair cut short. She felt uncomfortable in the short skirts of light-weight fabric common in her childhood. Mary's skirt was long and made of dark wool. As an adult Jenny rolls up shirt sleeves; Mary wore blouses with three-quarter length sleeves.

The eldest of Jenny's past-life children, Sonny, described his mother as a sturdy person of average height. Jenny recalls feeling too tall when she reached a height of 5'10" at age thirteen.

I found more physical similarities between Amanda and myself, as well as other members of my family. In the pictures Amanda's forehead is high, like mine. Our ears look similar. Most interesting, she has a large nose, similar to my mother's, grandmother's and great-grandmother's, the Marys of the family. Like Amanda, my mother was tall and slender in the 1940's.

Amanda carried herself well, and she impressed me as an intelligent, self-confident woman. When I shared my feelings with her daughter, Mrs. Jones said her family agreed. To them she was very special.

Receiving the pictures in the lunch-time mail, I finished eating, left them on the kitchen table, and returned to the computer. After spending an hour working on SHADOWS ON MY MIND I sensed a presence in the house. It was warm, like my mother's when she was near. I reminded myself she was not visiting, and I was alone. Thinking of the pictures I concluded it must be Amanda. Her warmth permeated the house all day, uplifting me. What a wonderful birthday present!

I was born in 1946, and when I thought about it synchronicity became apparent. The year was 1992, the one hundredth anniversary of Amanda's birth. I had received photographs of her on my 46th birthday, and she had died in 1946. More curious facts came to light four days after the pictures arrived. I called Mrs. Jones to thank her for the photographs and to ask more questions about her mother. Since

141

she had been unable to complete the questionnaire I decided to get the most important information by telephone.

We talked about her mother's appearance, and I found similarities between the elder Amanda and myself. She had dressed fashionably for the office, and she had kept herself slender. I had a few pounds to lose, but I had been slim as a young woman and wore the latest style clothing.

With regard to facial features and coloring it seemed we resembled one another only in our foreheads and ears. It took several hours before I made the connection between Amanda's black hair and my birthmark. I have black eyebrows and lashes, uncommon in redheads, and had been born a strawberry blond **with a streak of black down the back of my head.** By age ten the streak had turned to gray. Amanda would have been sixty-three by then, and likely to have gray in her hair. This connected us. Another resonant feature is in our hairlines. Amanda's had a well-formed widow's peak, and I have an inverted widow's peak. I have always admired dark hair and widow's peaks, and for a long time I hid my hairline by wearing bangs or parting my hair on the side. I married a black-haired man with a widow's peak, and our son has one as well.

Another physical link with Amanda Randall is an "R" on my left thigh, formed by broken capillaries. I first noticed the formation in my 20's, when dating a man whose last name began with "R". Considering this a sign we would marry, I was puzzled as well as hurt when we broke up.

Amanda and I have other characteristics in common, among them strong bonds with our sisters. I sensed Amanda had been blessed with three sisters. Mrs. Jones confirmed it. Her mother came from a family of six children; there had been two sons and four daughters. My family has two sons and five daughters. I am the eldest, but Amanda had been the fifth child, born between sisters Marie and Anna, with whom she had been close. My given name is Mary Ann, which is not surprising as a person chooses her name before birth. (3) Amanda would have liked this link with her sisters. I picked Marie as part of my pen name because I have always considered it special, and I'm more comfortable being known as "Marie" than as "Mary".

In addition to her sisters, Amanda had a lot of other friends and got along well with everyone, according to her daughter. Mrs. Jones wrote: "(She) was a wonderful, sweet person, never had a bad word to say about anyone. (She) had many friends, was very well liked by so many people. (She) had a wonderful repore (sic) with her sisters."

I have made many friends over the years, keeping them for long periods of time. I still see classmates from high school. Gossiping is one of my faults, but I look for positive rather than negative qualities in people.

Amanda and I have both made sacrifices for our families. She turned down an out-of-state promotion because she thought the move would disrupt her family. At the time the younger Amanda and her brother had been in junior high school, and they would have had to leave their friends. Although I have been tempted to take an outside job, I have stayed at home with my hyperactive son.

Amanda and I share perfectionism. In the observation of her daughter, she kept their four-room flat immaculate, despite working full-time in an office. Amanda must have led a stressful life. She arose early in the morning to catch the street car to work, put in a full day, then hurried home to make dinner. Before the 1950's little prepared food was available in grocery stores, and Amanda cooked dinner for her family every night. Mrs. Jones considered her mother a good cook, but she served mostly meat and potatoes, her father's preference. On Friday the family had fish because Mr. Randall had come from a Catholic background. The younger Amanda helped her mother by paring potatoes, but Mother did nearly everything else.

Nor were weekends relaxing. Amanda never had a washing machine, and linens and clothing went to a wet wash. Laundry returned in a bag, damp and wrinkled. It took all day Saturday to iron it, an exhausting job. Other arduous chores included grocery shopping without a car, and housecleaning without a vacuum cleaner.

Still Amanda took the time to visit friends in the evening, and the Saturday night pinochle games with her sister and their children were the highlight of the week. Amanda and Marie spoke Danish, and Marie's children knew the language well, but the younger Amanda had never wanted to learn.

Sundays Amanda and her brother Jim attended the Baptist church, but her mother wasn't a church goer and only appeared at special events. I imagine Mother cooked or did housework while they were gone.

Mrs. Jones remarked her mother's fussiness about the home may have led to her early death from a bleeding ulcer. Jim, discharged by the army, returned from California on Sunday, the day the bleeding started. Amanda had worked hard to get her home in order and was very tired. The first hemorrhage started just before Jim arrived, but she was so eager to see him she refused to go to the hospital. Her daughter worried. In order to watch her mother the younger Amanda had insisted she sleep in the same bedroom. At 2:00 Monday morning her mother began to hemorrhage again, from both her mouth and rectum. An ambulance rushed her to the hospital. Mrs. Jones thought her mother might have received better care at the university-affiliated hospital, but her father insisted she go to St. John's. She received a lot of blood (It took 25 of her daughter's coworkers to replace it.), but Amanda died the next morning at about 6:00.

What a shock for her daughter, present when she passed away. The younger Amanda thought the nun insensitive when she placed a sheet over her mother's head without mentioning her passing.

I still remember the last scene from Amanda's life. She was uncomfortable--her body felt hot, and she couldn't breathe. Perhaps the nun pulled the sheet over her head too soon.

Amanda didn't expect to die. She was only fifty-three, and probably looking forward to her daughter's wedding, and grandchildren. She may have had a weakness for ulcers, which her son Jim has today. Her daughter has ulcerative colitis, another disease aggravated by stress.

I agree with Mrs. Jones that her mother's perfectionism may have contributed to her premature death. A perfectionist lives with a lot of pressure, and disorders such as ulcers, migraines, and colitis are stress-related. Germs might cause ulcers, but emotional strain can aggravate them as well as contribute to migraine headaches, which Amanda had in addition to an ulcer. Although I have never experienced a migraine headache or been diagnosed with colitis, when I am nervous my intestines become irritated. I have always feared ulcers and tried to calm myself to avoid developing them. This can be explained by perfectionist tendencies, and vulnerability because of my past-life experience.

Amanda was fussy about her home, maybe because of her Danish background. When I visited Denmark everything seemed pristine, especially the homes.

My perfectionism extends beyond our house, where my husband complains I am "too clean", to hobbies like sewing, where I rip out a lot of seams. My mother also took extra care in sewing, so I may have learned this from her. She was not a neat housekeeper, however, and my cleanliness could be a reaction to growing up in a disorganized household. My behavior is likely the result of both my past life and my upbringing, and Amanda's was probably as well.

My most intense fear may have more to do with living on a farm, where Grandpa killed hawks and chickens pecked us, than to a past life. At times birds of prey, particularly eagles, have terrified me. Because of White Cloud's death I had thought Amanda shared this fear, but Mrs. Jones said her mother was only frightened of snakes. Snakes don't bother me, unless I suspect they are poisonous.

As I spoke with Mrs. Jones I became aware of much synchronicity between her life and mine; in fact I have as much in common with her as I do with her mother. Mrs. Jones and I were both older than the usual bride. She was married at 26, five days after I was born. I was 27 when Nat and I took our vows. Both Mrs. Jones and I were wed in a Congregational church, the choice of our husbands. Each of us gave birth to sons at the age of 37. She calls hers Cliff, which has five letters, like my son's name, Colin. Mrs. Jones has two older children, a son and daughter, born close together, like those of the Anna of my regressions.

Mrs. Jones and I are both avid readers, and we knit. I was a teacher, and she a teacher's aide for several years. Each of us enjoys working with students. Mrs. Jones attends a book discussion group and is past president of a woman's club. I have run a writers' group for thirteen years, and was co-president of a woman's club.

The younger Amanda and I also show similarities in our personalities. We are both sensitive and sentimental, but we don't let emotions run our lives. Relationships with our families are of great importance. We are both tolerant, open minded.

Each of us enjoys the water. I have never lived far from a lake or river, and Mrs. Jones has lived much of her life near the ocean. She had a home at Marshall Pointe during my hypnotic regressions, and when I visited the area it seemed familiar.

I believe I made telepathic contact with Mrs. Jones, rather than her mother, during hypnosis. The elder Amanda had lived with her family in a beach cottage for two years during the 1940's, but it was not at Marshall Pointe.

Mrs. Jones met her husband at the beach cottage. Was this the foundation for the hypnotic regression story of Anna, who lived with her husband and three children in a cottage at Marshall Place?

Maybe the psychic connection with Mrs. Jones was easy to make because of our similarity. How much this has to do with the elder Amanda I don't know, but I suspect Mrs. Jones has some of her mother's traits. The fact they have the same first name probably means similar personality characteristics. (4)

There is synchronicity between Mrs. Jones' brother and my family. He and my younger brother have the same name, Jim, and my sister Renee and Jim's wife have the same first name. Like me, Jim is a writer; he has been a columnist at a local newspaper for many years.

Perhaps the elder Amanda and I have less in common than I had expected because she spent most of her life prior to World War II., in a different world than we know today. Amanda never had a washing machine, nor a vacuum cleaner. The family didn't own a car and depended upon trolleys.

During the great depression Amanda's husband was out of work, then labored for the Department of Public Works. Amanda supported her family by working as a stenographer for a large grocery chain.   Except for brief periods of unemployment, my husband has worked as a statistician, and I haven't had to help support our family.

Unlike Amanda, I have never been able to type well, which I blame on poor coordination. It is fortunate I live in the computer age; otherwise I would have to hire someone to type my manuscripts. As it stands, I am likely to spend the remainder of my working life at a computer, as Amanda spent hers at a typewriter.

Amanda and I didn't have common hobbies or diversions, but we lived in different eras, and I have more leisure time. Her daughter and I are able to read and knit, and her son was able to find time to write even before he retired. While I watch t.v., Amanda played pinochle. My husband and I would rather see a play than attend a boxing match as Amanda and her husband did. But my grandmother also enjoyed boxing, which she watched on television. If Amanda had lived into the 1950's, when sets were owned by more people, she might have done the same.

The reason Grandma and Amanda enjoyed watching fights may have been out of frustration. They lived before the sexual revolution and weren't expected to be aggressive.   Watching boxing was an outlet for them, an acceptable way of handling their tensions.

Viewing boxing was a good way for Amanda to relieve the considerable stress in her life. Too often she kept her anxiety within, and it turned against her, contributing to ulcers and migraines.

It appears Amanda tried to be the perfect wife, mother, and friend. She doted on Jake, waiting upon him "hand and foot". Amanda sacrificed for her family, refusing a promotion and taking time off work to spend a winter at a health farm with her sickly son. She was close to her sisters and visited her many friends. It wasn't likely Amanda took time to care for herself, however, which probably resulted in her premature death.

Her daughter realized this. She told me her mother hadn't had the best medical care; she had never seen a specialist. The younger Amanda vowed she would have the best doctors when she had her babies, and afterward, and she has kept this promise to herself.

The most important lesson I learned from Amanda is to take care of myself. I began in college. Unlike some of my fellow students, I refused to overload myself with too many courses or take a job for more than a few hours a week. I quit my first full-time job, as a social worker, because of stomach aches and sleeping problems. When I found Mrs. Jones and discovered Amanda had died from a bleeding ulcer after working hard to make her home "perfect" for her son's homecoming, the message hit harder than ever. I have decided to spend my time and energy on the two things that matter most to me--my family and my writing. Taking a full-time job would likely impair my ability in one or both, and my health would suffer if I tried to do all of them well.

I'm sorry Amanda didn't live to see her children's weddings, or her grandchildren. In her last moments, when she knew death was inevitable, she likely felt cheated. This may have been why she was reborn in only three months. Dr. Stevenson believes those who feel incomplete at death, thinking they are entitled to a longer life, may have a craving for rebirth, which leads to quicker reincarnation. (5)

I would have liked Amanda, and I feel good about my association with the fine person she was. Learning about a previous personality by talking with someone who knew her is a rare experience, and I feel privileged. My life has been enriched by the knowledge of past lives and psychic experiences, and I now have a better understanding of who I am and why.

Once I was bitter about growing up on a farm, poor and isolated. Now I see the reasons for it. I learned humility and self-reliance, and to value relationships over material things. Although we lacked money my parents were more honest than most people, and my siblings and I understand the importance of ethics, which gives us a good foundation.

I was depressed when I couldn't find a permanent, full-time teaching position. I now know why--I was destined to become a writer. Some write while pursuing another career, but I also wanted a home and family, and juggling all three would have been too much for me.   My son has Attention Deficit Hyperactivity Disorder, and I need to spend much of my time caring for him.

In helping him I discovered the same disorder in myself. Daydreaming makes me a slow reader. I'm not efficient at the keyboard because of poor coordination, which often goes along with A.D.H.D. So do mood swings, and these are the hardest of any of the symptoms for me to manage. On the positive side, to compensate for my focusing problem I have learned to superconcentrate, and this may facilitate hypnosis and visualization. Attention to extraneous sights, sounds, and smells others miss makes me a good observer, and a better writer.

Like many others, I have faced substantial obstacles. Since the growth set in motion by my dream of Mohari, however, I have discovered gifts, accepted limitations, and come to understand preferences.   All have helped me deal more effectively with life.

As a child my light skin, with its tendency to burn in the sun, was difficult to accept. Over time I resigned myself to the pain, headaches, and disorientation when my skin burned, but deep inside I felt something was wrong. Skin was supposed to tan, especially my skin. In desperation I tried different types of tanning lotions, even a sunless one, but it streaked my skin orange, making me appear freakish. It was not until Colin was born with it that I saw beauty in ivory skin.

I have always felt dark hair is attractive, and prefer men with coloring darker than my own. I married Nat, who is half Filipino. He has black hair and gets wonderful tans.

Amanda had been able to get a dark tan. Pride showed in her daughter's voice when she told me of the ability of her family to turn brown in summer. Maybe Amanda had been too proud of her skin, and a life as a light-skinned person was necessary for balance. Among other reasons, my parents might have been chosen for their light skin.

In nearly all cases of suspected reincarnation Stevenson (6) has found connections between previous and current personalities. Many times people return to the same family; a man may be reborn as his grandson. In other cases the families are good friends. A previous personality died near the birth place of the present one in some, and in others one of the parents of the current person visited the community or place of death of the previous person around the time of the current person's conception. In some instances the current and previous personalities lived within 25 kilometers of one another; in others members of the previous person's family had some connection with the present person's community.

I have found evidence for none of the above. Amanda and I are not blood relatives, nor did our families know one another. My parents never visited New England, where Amanda died. I was born in Michigan, and Mrs. Jones knows of no connection between her family and my state. The same is true in Jenny Cockell's case; in her book she cited no evidence of a link between Mary Sutton's family and hers.

Our situation requires another explanation. I understand reincarnating entities choose their parents--they are not reborn at random. I believe my parents were selected in part for their light skin. Another factor was their religion: they were Catholic.

Amanda's husband was Catholic, but like me she did not attend church on a regular basis. Religion caused conflict in the family, and Mr. Randall returned to the Catholic church shortly after his wife's death. It may be Amanda chose to grow up Catholic to experience her husband's faith and to understand his commitment to it.

Another reason she opted to be reborn to my parents might be she knew they would raise a number of daughters. Amanda had been close to her sisters, especially to Marie, and she probably wanted the companionship of girls.

Entry into my family seemed set up for her, as my parents had decided to call their first-born daughter Mary Ann. My father's mother and paternal grandmother were named Anna, and there were three generations of Marys on my mother's side of the family. The name Mary Ann was chosen long before my mother became pregnant with me. Amanda died about six months after my conception, so it is unlikely she influenced their choice. Born between sisters Marie and Anna, whom she loved,

Amanda likely wanted the name Mary Ann in her next incarnation.

Finally, she "fit into" my family with her large nose, blue eyes, big hands and tall, slender build. Some of my mother's relatives have dark hair and tan well.

Whatever the reasons, I am grateful for the connection with Amanda. Part of a greater consciousness, we each constitute one of its many facets, like those of a gem. Time and space do not affect this entity.

One part can experience another facet as separate, which explains why I sensed Amanda's presence in the kitchen, while I was in the study, and why I saw the hospitalized woman in my childhood image. It also explains how I experienced the woman's feelings in the dream, at the same time I looked down on her and Mohari. Seeing past-life occurrences from two points of view, that of the person experiencing the event and that of an onlooker, is not unusual in past-life regressions during hypnosis, according to Dr. Moody. (7) I believe this is also true in dreams and spontaneous recollections.

Mohari and Anna may be two more facets of the entity of which Amanda and I are part. If this is so we are all true soul mates, and this explains the great attraction both the woman and I had toward Mohari, our yang, or male aspect.

Mohari and the woman could have lived in the past, in a different world, or maybe they have yet to exist. I may have created them to fill in for the lost memories of Amanda. Some would call that fantasy, others an alternate or parallel universe.

I learned more about Amanda when I traveled to New England in October of 1996. My mother had succumbed to cancer on July third of that year. I made the trip in part because of a message from her.

Three types of unusual experiences occurred around the time of her death. The first puzzled me. On Thursday, July third, the day Mom passed away, I awakened with an ache in my abdomen. I curled up, bending my back in reaction to the pain. There is a strong energy connection between mother and child, and the psychic umbilicus enables them to stay in contact after birth. The cord is torn when a relationship ends, sometimes causing much pain. (8) As I suffered I wondered if Mom had passed away. When the ache left I called Terri. Mom was still holding onto life.

I thought of her, dying. With the aid of Hospice workers we were able to keep her at her home, as she requested. My sister Terri, an experienced nurse with cancer patients, had come from Virginia. On Wednesday she told Sandy and me Mom had only hours to live. "Oh no," I wailed. I knew Mom was dying, but didn't think she would go that fast. She had only been home four days, and we needed more time with her. That evening, hoping to cheer Mom in her last hours, I played "Oklahoma", one of her favorite movies. When Mom acknowledged she heard the music my spirit lifted.

Mom didn't die that night. With a promise to return later on Thursday, I left after midnight, when the Hospice aide arrived. "Phantom of the Opera" filled my car on the way home; the music engaged me, helping control the sorrow.

The phone rang as I prepared to leave the house Thursday. Terri informed me Mom had passed away. Frustrated I had been unable to be with her in the last moments of her life, I wept.

In my grief I recalled the pain earlier that day. Had an invisible link between Mom and me been severed?

Over the following days the evidence for a broken connection mounted. In the wee hours of many mornings I awoke confused about where I was. Was I at Mom's, at home, or somewhere else? One morning I switched on my bedside lamp in panic. Finding myself at home I returned to a troubled sleep. After a number of weeks turning on a light was no longer necessary. I was content to gaze at dimly lit walls, assuring myself I was safe in my bedroom. Six months after Mom left us I occasionally awakened disoriented, but by then I had become accustomed to it. The fear had waned; however, I still felt cut loose, as if floating in a mysterious way.

Although I was grateful Mom had been released from a life of pain, her passing left me with an empty feeling. The second kind of extraordinary experiences connected with Mom were her messages, bringing comfort, reassuring me she still existed.

Sometimes they came in dreams. Shortly after her funeral I dreamed she lay on the kitchen floor of her house. My sister Renee and I helped her pale body up, and like a zombie she walked across the room. Mom never spoke, but she came to the door when her remaining daughters arrived. Sandy gasped when she saw Mom, who was supposed to be dead. I remained calm as I let in my sisters, and they kept their composure. We went to the living room to divide Mom's jewelry, linens, and other items.

Then I decided to take a picture for SHADOWS ON MY MIND. Terri had gone to the kitchen, and I followed, to borrow her camera.

When I returned Mom was leaving in an old-fashioned white bus, designed like a carriage. Before I could protest she was gone. I felt frustrated, but glad she had visited us.

The third kind of occurrences seemed magical. Mom loved butterflies, and she crocheted them for refrigerator magnets. One weekend, as I cleaned her house, my husband called and told me a large Swallowtail had come to the back entrance of our home. When Colin opened the door it flew in, and he put it into a jar. Large butterflies are rarely found in our vicinity, yet that fall another showed itself at a neighbor's kitchen window. Shortly before my New England trip I visited the home to speak about reincarnation. One of the sons of the family was writing a college paper on the subject. As my evening visit drew to a close a Monarch butterfly appeared at the darkened window. Was it my mother revealing herself? Before her death I had informed her spirits could take the form of animals, including insects.

I often sense Mom's presence, mostly in my mind. Not long after her death she sent me an important message. "Amanda is awful sick," came to me. I took it as a warning to visit my past-life daughter before time ran out for us.

It took months to make Mom's house presentable, but by mid-October it was ready to show prospective buyers, before snow and ice discouraged them. My brother and I listed the farm with our cousin's real estate agency. Giving up our home, after it had nurtured four generations of Paces, made the family sad, but none of us was in a position to keep it. Making travel plans took my mind off the inevitable sale.

I dialed Amanda's number. Having spoken with her four years before, I was surprized when a man answered the phone. He knew   nothing of Amanda. My first thought was she was dead. No, I said to myself, that couldn't be, not before I met her face-to-face.

Before calling directory assistance I needed reassurance. If she had passed away I wanted to hear it from my friend in the New England city where Amanda lived.

Since we had met on my first trip to New England, Elaine and I had corresponded. Hoping she could help find Amanda, I called her. She promised to contact acquaintances who knew Mrs. Jones. That evening, after I returned from my writers' group, Nat gave me a message from Elaine.

Amanda had undergone surgery for a brain tumor the previous spring. She had moved from her condominium to a mother-in-law apartment in the home of friends. Relieved she was alive, I prayed she was well enough to see me. I summoned the courage to call her the next day. To my surprize she sounded healthy on the phone. It seemed Elaine had gotten distorted information about Mr. Jones' condition. Amanda explained she had collapsed in the main part of the house where she lived, while the owners vacationed.   Fortunately, she regained consciousness after twenty minutes and made her way to the apartment. When Amanda told her son about the incident he insisted she see her doctor. Two days later she had surgery to remove a blood clot on her brain. At first the surgeon started the operation on the wrong side of her head, so Amanda has two sets of indentations in her forehead.

Amanda's invitation to stay at her apartment pleased me. She assured me it would be good for her to have a guest. Excited, I called a travel agent to make arrangements.

To my disappointment, I found flying would be expensive if I made a reservation less than two weeks in advance. I didn't want to wait that long as the weather in the north turns cold, and sometimes snowy, in November. Travel by train provided another option.   Amtrack was much less expensive, and I enjoyed riding the rails.

On October 22, 1996, I began my journey in Detroit. Nat drove me to the train station where I boarded a bus for Toledo, Ohio. At about 12:30 a.m. the train left, bound for Washington D.C.

When I entered the train a woman lay sleeping across my assigned seat as well as her own. Feelings of guilt came when I displaced her, but she did not appear to resent my intrusion. I stretched my legs, becoming somewhat comfortable.   Sleep overtook me, only to be interrupted by the flashing red "no smoking" sign and its accompanying jingle. Each time the train stopped the message awakened me. Morning found me groggy.

My seat mate, a large middle-aged woman, informed me of a ladies lounge at the end of the next car. I closed my eyes and rested until 9:00 a.m., when Judy said no one was waiting to use it.

After grooming myself in the small but comfortable lounge, I made my way to the snack bar, where I purchased yogurt, a bagel and juice. The observation area upstairs beckoned me. There I spent some of the best moments of my trip. The train wound its way through woods where the trees displayed the colors of autumn--reds, golds, oranges, and browns. At times streams flowed beside the tracks; over slopes and rocks they meandered. The water looked clear enough to drink in some places, but streams emptied into muddy rivers along the way. Not long before the Pennsylvania region had been flooded. Remnants littered the ground--a sofa, a chair, a tire. Rags, which might have been clothing, hung in trees.

Soon a steward announced lunch in the dining car. Still full from my late breakfast, I declined. The Washington station was not far away. Or so I thought. The train arrived more than a hour late, and passengers barely had time to make the connection to New England. I ate a granola bar on the second train.

Debris on the tracks in Philadelphia disabled the engine, and we stopped outside the station. I hoped nothing else would disrupt the trip. Elaine and her husband would await a call when I reached my destination.

Tired from a poor night's sleep, I curled up on my seat and the empty one beside me. My trench coat substituted for a blanket as we waited for a replacement engine. In the darkened train I napped.

When I awakened the train was nearly ready to leave the station. Refreshed, excitement filled me. At last I was going to meet my past-life daughter.

Outside New York City a steward helped a disabled woman from a wheel chair onto the train. I moved over, and she occupied my former aisle seat. We talked of her family problems and my writing for the remainder of the trip.

At the train station I called Elaine, then paced the floor in anticipation of my meeting Amanda. When Elaine and her husband were due I slipped out of the station, into the rainy night. In a short time they arrived. I was happy to see them again, and to ride in their comfortable sedan to Amanda's apartment.

Mixed emotions surfaced on the way to the northern suburb. I felt excited, yet apprehensive. My worst fear was rejection. What if Mrs. Jones were cold to me? No, I told myself, she had always been friendly on the phone. My claim her mother was my past personality is extraordinary, but Amanda has never uttered a critical word about my belief. She hasn't told me whether she accepts reincarnation or not. I am reluctant to ask, for fear the question will embarrass her, or the answer will disturb me.

As the car pulled into the driveway anxiety nearly took over. For a second I wanted to escape the vehicle and run away. But that would have meant a wasted trip. I needed to see Amanda not only for my book, but for myself. After waiting seventeen years to meet her, I had to go through with it.

To my surprize an outpouring of love emanated from me when I met the slender white-haired lady. Joy overtook me as we embraced, and I murmured "I love you". Amanda hugged me back but did not respond to my words. Shortly after our greeting I asked Elaine's husband to take a picture of Amanda, Elaine, and me, then one of Amanda and me. He and Elaine stayed for a brief chat. Amanda recalled meeting Elaine in the past, but Elaine had no such recollection. In a few minutes they left me alone with Amanda.

Feeling awkward, I looked about the living room. The blue sofa and the round table with the floral print cloth reminded me of home. Like me, Amanda decorated with flowers and displayed greeting cards. She had celebrated a birthday the day before I called her. Ten days later her cards remained on the round table.

"Are you hungry?" Amanda reclaimed my attention. I detected concern in her voice.

"A little," I admitted. I had only eaten a sandwich and snacks on the train, but I didn't want to trouble her.

She hesitated. "Would zucchini bread be all right?"

"Zucchini bread?" I asked, defusing the tension within. "Did you make it?

"Yes."

"I make it too." Smiling, I examined the rose pattern on her silverware. "You know we have a lot in common. My silverware has roses too." I turned toward the living room. "I also have a blue sofa, and pink flowers in my dining room."

After I enjoyed her warm zucchini bread and tea Amanda asked me to refresh her memory about my relationship with her mother. I reminded her of the hypnotic regressions, where I had obtained her parents' names and their city. On my first visit, in October of 1979, her former landlord gave me Amanda's married name, and I called her. What convinced me her mother and I were connected was the similarity of her mother's death scene (as Amanda had reported it) and the death scene I recall from infancy. The Catholic hospital with my daughter at my side as I lay dying is still a vivid memory.

Because I remembered the daughter wearing a scarf over her head, I purchased a floral silk square as a hostess gift for Amanda. She was happy to receive it, and she saved the wrap, as I do on special occasions.

The last time we had been together she was grieving over her mother; this time we both grieved the deaths of loved ones-- my mother and Amanda's daughter. In 1995 Amanda had lost

Penny to liver cancer. In her last month of life doctors found cancer in Mom's liver, another parallel.

Meaningful coincidences connecting Amanda and me abound, from food and decorating choices, to common interests. Like me, Amanda spends considerable time reading, as evidenced by the many books in her home. We both enjoy knitting. Even our husbands look alike.

A picture of Lyle, now deceased, graced a shelf in Amanda's living room. Like Nat, he had an oval face, thick eyebrows, a full mouth, and dark hair.

Amanda presented other pictures before bedtime, including portraits of her mother and aunts when they were young. These pictures gave me a clearer view of her mother's features than the snapshots had afforded. The elder Amanda, with big eyes and thick wavy hair, had been attractive in her youth. She and I have nearly identical noses and ear lobes, and light-colored eyes. Hers were bright blue, and mine are green. Like the elder Amanda, I have thick, wavy hair, but mine is auburn, instead of black. Our foreheads are high, but Amanda's face is more oval than mine. Her sister Anna and I have squarish faces and full lips, in contrast to Amanda's thin ones. Even as a child, Amanda had a look of serenity, as if she were content with herself. Friends have remarked I seem peaceful.

I asked my hostess for permission to copy the pictures the next day, and she said I could take them home. She knew I would return them. I smiled, thanking her, and I couldn't express my joy with her trusting me to care for irreplaceable family photographs.

Tired from the nearly twenty-four hour trip, I felt relieved when Amanda suggested we retire. She showed me to the bedroom and loaned me a comfortable robe, as I was traveling light and had none. I didn't fall asleep immediately, for excitement filled me. The next day I would see the grave of my past-life identity. Would I feel her presence?

Thursday, October 24, dawned bright and sunny. I awakened before Amanda but lay in bed waiting for her to rise and use the apartment's only bathroom. While I dressed she prepared breakfast.

Hot oatmeal, toast, and juice welcomed me when I arrived in the kitchen. Their familiarity comforted me; I often enjoyed instant oatmeal and juice, and sometimes toast, on cool mornings.

After breakfast Amanda appeared in a dark turtleneck and stirrup pants, similar to my own outfit. I had on a dark green mock turtleneck shirt and stretch pants. I had left my stirrup pants at home. Perhaps Amanda's mother would have worn similar clothing, had she been with us. Later that day Amanda pointed out a picture of her mother in dark slacks and a dressy blouse. Pearls and black patent high heels completed her outfit. The photograph was from the 1940's, when women wearing pants in public elicited disapproval. Amanda's mother had been brave to disregard convention.

Totally at ease, I talked with Amanda, and we snacked on crackers while waiting for her friend Dolores to take us to the cemetery. Dolores had called offering Amanda a ride to the library, which she had accepted as she had books to return. After her brain surgery, Amanda depended on family and friends for transportation. Dolores would drive us to the grave yard on the way to the library.

I enjoyed spending time with Dolores, a robust woman, with a keen sense of humor. She had known Amanda for many years, since they raised their families in the same neighborhood of the inner city. Passing a park on the way to the cemetery they reminisced about skating on the lagoon there. Then they talked about the old neighborhood, which we would drive through after we visited the cemetery.

The graveyard did not appear the way I had envisioned it. In my imagination numerous mature trees would darken it, and many old tombstones, some with barely visible names and dates, would stand in long rows. I expected a somber atmosphere, despite the sunny day.

Instead, the cemetery impressed me as a quiet open space. It evoked no strong emotion. Few trees grew in the area, and the tombstones seemed relatively new. Many grave sites remained empty. I failed to comprehend the unusual occurrence there until weeks later.

As we looked for her parents' graves Amanda confided the family could not afford a headstone at the time of her mother's death. Her parents' resting place had only markers, flush with the ground. We found the spot using a nearby headstone, familiar to Amanda, as a point of reference.

For a moment I stood before the graves, concentrating on those buried below. I hoped to feel a presence, but to my disappointment, none was detected. Overgrown grass had begun to cover both Jake's and Amanda's markers. Their daughter and her friend started tearing out the grass, so I could read the stones. I knelt on the ground to help them.

I was only vaguely aware of it at first, but arising to take a picture of Amanda's marker I became concerned. A shadow covered a little over half the stone and the grass surrounding it. I looked around to determine its source, and was amazed to find none. No tree grew close enough to cast the shadow that early autumn afternoon. The sky was clear blue, without a cloud, and no aircraft flew overhead. As the shadow was straight and long, like that of a tree, no human could have cast it. Hoping it would not obscure the carvings on the stones, I took pictures.

Without a thought about the shadow's significance, I left the cemetery with Amanda and Dolores, bound for the central city where they had lived in the 1940's.

Not until December did I recognize the importance of the shadow. Terri and I spent three days in the old homestead, to be sold the next month. The house had been filled with clutter; Mom had kept everything, including sheet music from the 1930's, greeting cards from the 1940's on, and magazines from the 1950's to 1996. Betty lives in Indiana, Terri in Virginia, and Sandy had returned to teaching in August. I, as trustee, had spent many fall weekends completing the cleaning.

Terri thanked me warmly. For the first time in years the house looked like a home, and she slept better in it than she ever had before. Terri, studying to be a nurse practitioner, had come on break for closure. She looked through the antiques, taking dishes, linens, an Eastlake baby crib, and two old dressers. One, our grandfather's wedding gift, had been in the family since

1899. An amateur photographer, Terri strolled about the farm taking pictures.

I showed her the photos from my New England trip. She made no comments on the pictures of Elaine, Amanda and me, but the shadow on the grave marker excited her, and she remarked, "That's spooky! It ought to be on the cover of your book!"

I hadn't thought of that. When the pictures came back from the processor I was eager to see if the shadow appeared on the grave marker, but I was more concerned about the photos of Amanda and me. Fortunately, they all came out well. I thought little about the shadow until Terri made me aware of its gravity.

I brought the pictures of my trip to the February writers' meeting. After I had related my experience, Victoria, a Reiki practitioner, told me she had been shocked when one of her clients reported a shadow over her recently deceased mother's grave. This occurred on cloudy day, when no other shadows were visible. Perhaps the phenomenon is more common than I had realized.

What could have caused it? I can think of three possibilities. First, I could have created it--how, I do not know. Humans use only a small amount of their brain potential. The apparatus for psi, extrasensory perception and psychokinesis is likely present, ready to be tapped. My connection with Amanda, whose remains lay below me, might have been sufficient to trigger the shadow.

To the ancients sunbeams and shadows were highly significant. They designed stones and mounds of earth to show the time of day as well as seasonal changes. At Stonehenge the manipulation of light and shadow may have played a role in religious rituals.

To me, the graveyard shadow symbolizes life and death. More than half the marker was covered in darkness, meaning most of my lifetimes are in the past. The light portion of the stone represents the present and what is to come, my current life and those in the future.

Second and third explanations of the shadow concern forces outside myself. Perhaps and angel or spirit guide created the phenomenon to inform me I am moving in the right spiritual direction, encouraging me to pursue past lives.

Third among possibilities is the remote chance of extraterrestrial involvement. Space craft and apparent celestial illusions have been seen with appearances of the Virgin Mary. At Fatima, Portugal, on October 13, 1917, the Virgin showed herself to three shepherd children, but the crowd of 50,000 could not see her. They did, however, see the sun spin and begin to plunge toward Earth, three times. (9)

In my dreams the spirit Mohari told me his people have been watching Earth, aiding in human evolution, both physical and spiritual. From reading accounts of extraterrestrial contacts I learned alien visitors believe in reincarnation, including those who abduct people. Crop circles and increased UFO activity may mean other intelligent beings are begging us to acknowledge them. Could the graveyard shadow be one more sign of their presence?

Those who have encountered UFO's know about the paranormal. I believe all of us have had some psychic experiences; if we accept them and consider their meaning, we can learn much. Many deny the unexplained, pushing it to the backs of their minds. I have always paid attention to the unusual, pondering it, enjoying the mystery. The exploration of shadows, the shadows on my mind, has fascinated me. Although phenomena such as e.s.p. are rare and fleeting for most of us, I consider them a normal part of living which enriches us when we focus on them.

Chapter Ten

Past Lives and Spiritual Growth

As a young woman I had prayed for faith, to a God I didn't know existed. In time my prayers were answered, but in a way I had never expected--I came to believe in reincarnation, an idea that had been foreign to me.

It was a slow process, but after the hypnotic regressions, after finding Amanda Jones, I couldn't deny the validity of reincarnation. I had no other explanation for the early images of the hospitalized woman, her daughter, and the nuns. At last I was liberated from the fear death marked the end of existence.

I am what Wade Roof, who wrote A GENERATION OF SEEKERS, (1) calls a seeker, a spiritual person, but not a church-goer. People like me trust our own experiences rather than the teachings of religious authorities. Each person must follow her own inclinations in finding God. Spiritual growth, healing, and living in harmony with the environment are important to us.

Although I'm not certain Christ is the son of God as Christianity teaches, he has always been special to me. Under hypnosis I made contact with him. In one session I saw myself as part of a crowd listening to him. I was close to the platform where he stood, and I could see only his feet and his long white robe, but I **knew** it was Jesus. Perhaps I saw myself in a past life, one which I have yet to explore, where I was a disciple. On another occasion I mentally conversed with Jesus while listening to an hypnosis tape. I asked his advice on a problem. He indicated I had to make up my own mind; he could not decide for me. This was somewhat disappointing, but knowing Jesus is there for me, that I can contact him when needed, makes me feel valued as an individual and helps me cope with life's trials and sorrows.   Seekers like me resemble the mystics of long ago, meditating and sometimes developing psychic powers. Reincarnation was, and is, often accepted by those who must find their own truth.

The independence of the mystics led to their persecution in the middle ages; the church felt threatened by those who didn't need it.   There is evidence early Christian Gnostics believed in reincarnation, but scholars and writers are reluctant to discuss it. Beginning in 553 A.D., belief in the preexistence of the soul on Earth was grounds for excommunication from the Catholic church.   During the middle ages hundreds of thousands of Christian reincarnationists succumbed in holy wars and inquisitions. (2)

As an independent thinker, reincarnation appeals to me, and it has enabled me to make sense of my life. It not only explains the death-bed images of my infancy, but my birth mark as well, the black streak in my strawberry blonde hair. Amanda had jet black hair according to her daughter.

In addition, reincarnation has helped explain my fears, particularly my life-long concern I would develop ulcers. Amanda died from a bleeding ulcer.

John, an 18th century sailor, drowned when he jumped from his ship. As a child this memory surfaced when I saw a sailor jump overboard on t.v., and I was so upset I ran from my grandparents' living room. As a college student on a Danish ship I considered jumping into the North Sea after my boyfriend had rejected me, showing John's continuing influence.

Ironically, a young man named Jørn, the Danish equivalent of John, rescued me and later invited me to his home. Years after the encounter I discovered the woman in my infant memory had Danish parents, and her brothers had been born in Denmark.

Reflecting on my past lives has enabled me to see a pattern of development.   The fact I had only thought of jumping overboard indicates spiritual progress since the life of John in the 1700's. From Amanda I learned to take care of myself; her inability to do so contributed to her premature death.

Jenny Cockell (3) benefitted from delving into her past life as Mary Sutton. From childhood on she had grieved for her lost family, and when an hypnotist agreed to work with her she learned more about Mary. However, during the course of the hypnotic regressions Jenny became obsessed with her search for the children left behind when their mother died. The stress exhausted her, and she needed medication for depression. Finding the children brought not only relief, but peace, and they have enriched her life.

Like Jenny's, my odyssey began with a dream. I was obsessed as well, only not with Amanda and her family, but with Mohari. He provided the motivation necessary to pursue my past lives, but, like Jenny, I suffered under the influence of hypnosis. Grieving for Mohari, yet fearing him at times, I had lost control of my life. Past life exploration can lead to spiritual growth, but I wouldn't recommend hypnotic regressions to anyone with mental or emotional problems.

Studying Amanda's life enabled me to see my strengths and weaknesses. I think pride is a major flaw which carried over from Amanda's life. Like her, I am proud of my appearance. She was slim, wore fashionable clothing and was likely pleased with the tans she could get in summer. My inability to get them has caused me a lot of pain, physically and emotionally.

Pride was at the root of Amanda's perfectionism in housekeeping. She may have chosen to be reborn to a woman who had trouble organizing her home in an attempt to overcome this excess, but it backfired. I became a "fussy" housekeeper.

It was my destructive son who led to my giving up a "perfect" home. Constantly cleaning and repairing the damage doesn't make sense as his impulsivity and temper tantrums persist.

Growing older, I take less pride in my appearance. When I was young and slim I could wear the latest fashions, but I have gained weight, and clothing isn't as important as it once was.

I believe past life influences should be included in personality theory, beside heredity and environment. They would help explain why people think and behave as they do, especially when fears of unknown origin are involved.

My fear of ulcers has no explanation in my current life, but Amanda died as a result of a bleeding ulcer. Birds are a source of more intense fear for me, but because Amanda was supposedly not afraid of them I am unsure this fear stems from a past life. From negative childhood experiences I have enough reasons to dislike birds. The worst incident was my Grandfather's killing a hawk and then nailing it to the door of an outbuilding; for years it was too painful to remember.

Some might say I was afraid of the hawk because of White Cloud's death. This is possible, but why did the fear stay with me, after I knew about the eagles killing him? Many therapists, including Dr. Brian Weiss, author of MANY LIVES, MANY MASTERS, (4) have been able to help patients overcome fears through hypnotic regressions to past lives. When a patient re-lives a traumatic event she generally loses the fear associated with it.

More effective in dispelling my fear of bald eagles are the post office displays of them in buildings as well as in advertizements on trucks, billboards, and in magazines. They have become so familiar I have little fear of eagles any more, and my feelings about other birds of prey are less troubling.

The fear of birds is a complex issue; whether or not it comes from a past life is difficult to determine. If it does it may be because I am more similar to White Cloud than Amanda was. Although we have past lives in common, we are separate individuals. Perhaps further hypnotic regressions will settle the question.

In my opinion, hypnosis can be a useful tool in the treatment of some phobias and other problems, but the past lives recalled by patients and others should be carefully considered. It is unlikely every fear originates in a previous life, and much information from past life regressions will probably never be substantiated. The only facts I could verify from the many sessions devoted to the life of Anna was Amanda's husband's name, the town in which they had lived in the 1940's, and the fact she had borne two sons and a daughter.

Perhaps I remembered the family's surname because it was "on the tip of my tongue" since childhood. As a preschooler I had argued with my father over our last name, thinking mine was longer. Randall has seven letters, and my maiden name has only four. Mr. Taylor coaxed "Randall" from me in two hypnotic sessions; I don't think he would have been successful if the information had not been close to consciousness.

The road atlas, with Marshall Pointe prominently displayed, jogged my memory, and under hypnosis I recalled the nearby town's name with ease. Mrs. Jones' living in the area at the time might have helped; while hypnotized I may have made telepathic contact with her. Similarities exist between her life and Anna's. Like Anna, the younger Amanda had met her husband at a beach cottage and given birth to two sons and a daughter.

Jenny Cockell began sketching maps as a child. Malahide, north of Dublin, drew her when she looked at a map of Ireland in her school atlas. She later discovered Mary Sutton had lived there.

Another trigger was a blonde, blue-eyed doll who looked like Mary's youngest child, Elizabeth. Jenny had given the doll the same name, but she was unable to remember the family's correct surname under hypnosis. Her mind apparently filled in "O'Neil".

Maybe I made up the story of Anna's life to compensate for my failure to recall the details of Amanda's. The science fiction tale was predictable because of my interest in the genre since childhood.

I believe Mohari is a discarnate, possibly an angel, sent to encourage me to write. His underlying message was: "Marie, you've waited long enough. Now it's time to write as you promised." (before birth) If he hadn't come to me, I would write to fulfill an inner need, but I wouldn't have possessed the motivation to complete a book.

I can only speculate about Mohari's history. He could have been embodied at one time; it's possible he was a previous personality of mine. He could also represent a future life.

Whether he and Anna are from the past or future, or exist in a parallel universe, their experiences have affected me. When their space craft collided with the mother ship they were killed. Because I feared "crashing into something" I didn't obtain my driver's license until age twenty-six. I have always driven carefully, and I have never been involved in a serious accident.

Mohari's influence on me has been much deeper and more significant than the above. The dream of Anna and him transformed my life. Near-death investigator Kenneth Ring (5) would call it a catalyst for spiritual awakening. Closeness to death is only one trigger for the experience of pure love and complete acceptance I felt in my dream. My transformation afterward included the recognition of psychic abilities, which Ring considers a by-product of spiritual development.

He believes near-death experiences may reflect a revolution of consciousness which could greatly alter mankind. Liberation from the fear of death would enable humanity to live naturally, joyously. I agree. Death is no longer frightening, as I know my spirit will last forever. I can now enjoy life. With greater serenity, I am more at home in the world than ever before.

Since enlightenment I know the workings of a higher power, the source of unconditional love and acceptance. I have experienced it in synchronicity, as when Nat and I found Dad. This showed us how people are connected with one another, while revealing an organizing source of energy as well. Sometimes I think the higher power is experimenting with us, seeking to know itself through us, as we are all connected, all one mind. Before we are born into a life our journey is planned by highly evolved spirits (Masters), but we make the final choices in our lives. When we fail to follow the plan designed to help us grow spiritually others, sometimes angels,sometimes fellow humans, keep us on track. They also protect us, rescuing us from premature death and other disasters.

We are all players on the stage of life. What we do affects all of creation. Because we are part of a higher power, not only our actions, but also our thoughts and feelings are important. We each possess great energy, and together we can accomplish nearly anything, including the transformation of the world.

After the dream and regressions I realized this and resolved to spend the rest of my life helping others and improving life on this planet. One of the reasons I wrote this book is to give people hope. Life does not end with death, and no matter how they have lived they will be given additional lives in order to develop spiritually.

More than anything else I wish to be the archetypal "wise old woman", advising others in many ways, helping them grow. Like White Cloud I want to be a peacemaker, to work with others to make the world a safer, more nurturing place. I have begun with prayers and visualization, and this has worked. I can likely mobilize energy in others as I sense a connection with everyone. This explains why visualizing a cure for sick people often helps them.

In July of 1992 I attended one of Benny Hinn's healing sessions. Both my mother and Sheila, the wife of a cousin, had cancer. So did Dana, a member of my writers' group, who had invited me to attend the session with her and her husband. I closed my eyes and felt one with the universe as I concentrated on healing Mom, Sheila, and others. To everyone's surprize Mom and Sheila recovered. Dana died in June of 1994.

Thinking Dana could take care of herself I hadn't concentrated on her at Hinn's session. When I discovered the cancer had spread to her liver guilt surfaced, and I sent white light and prayers to her every day for months. But Dana and I understood not everyone can be saved. At her memorial service she came into my mind, asking me to complete my book, for her as well as myself. Death had prevented her from writing the book I had inspired.

I often "feel" the spirits of living loved ones as well, particularly as we embrace. Sometimes I can almost "see" their auras. But the only aura I have actually experienced was Father Timothy's, on my sixteenth birthday.

This memory has taken on a new meaning since my enlightenment. I knew it contained an important message before, but I wasn't sure what it was. Now I see it in the context of a myth; it goes to the heart of human experience, illustrating the universal theme of redemption. It may be seen as the battle for a girl's soul between the powers of darkness (symbolized by the bat) and those of light (symbolized by the priest's aura).

The priest is human; he lusts for the girl, but she discourages him, and he relents. The girl's father slays the bat with his prayer book and places it in the usher's collection basket, symbolic of sacrifice. Then the girl sees the priest's beautiful white aura, showing his spirituality despite his sin. They are both saved.

THE END

NOTES

CHAPTER TWO
TRANSFORMATION

1. Richard Bucke, COSMIC CONSCIOUSNESS, New York, E.P. Dutton, 1967.

2. Richard Corriere and Joseph Hart, THE DREAM MAKERS: DISCOVERING YOUR BREAKTHROUGH DREAMS, New York, Funk and Wagnalls, 1977.

3. Gail Sheehy, PASSAGES: PREDICTABLE CRISES IN ADULT LIFE, New York, E.P. Dutton, 1977.

4. Carl Jung, THE BASIC WRITINGS OF C.G. JUNG, New York, Random House, The Modern Library, 1959, p. 40.

5. Jane Roberts, THE NATURE OF PERSONAL REALITY: A SETH BOOK, Englewood Cliffs, New Jersey, Prentice-Hall, Inc., 1976.

6. Jane Roberts, SETH SPEAKS: THE ETERNAL VALIDITY OF THE SOUL, Englewood Cliffs, New Jersey, Prentice-Hall, Inc., 1974.

7. Russell Targ and Harold E. Puthoff, MIND-REACH: SCIENTISTS LOOK AT PSYCHIC ABILITY, New York, Delacorte Press, Eleanor Friede, 1977.

8. Edith Fiore, THE UNQUIET DEAD, Garden City, N.Y., Doubleday and Company, Inc., 1987, p. 109. Psychologist Edith Fiore reported a client feeling earthbound entities "pushing down" heavily upon him. See Chapter 3 of SHADOWS ON MY MIND.

9. Paul Schilder, THE NATURE OF HYPNOSIS, New York, International Universities Press, Inc., 1956, p. 73.

10. Raymond A. Moody Jr., COMING BACK: A PSYCHIATRIST EXPLORES PAST-LIFE JOURNEYS, New York, Bantam Books, 1991, pp. 143 and 145.

11. Jenny Cockell, ACROSS TIME AND DEATH: A MOTHER'S SEARCH FOR HER PAST LIFE CHILDREN, New York, Simon & Schuster, Fireside, 1994, p. 104.

12. Ibid, P. 38.

13. Morey Bernstein, THE SEARCH FOR BRIDEY MURPHY, new edit., New York, Doubleday, 1989.

14. John F. Kihlstrom, "Hypnosis", in ANN. REV. PSYCHOL., 36:385-418, 1985, pp. 399-400.

15. Ibid, p. 401.

16. Michael A. Thalbourne, "Some Correlates of Belief in Psychical Phenomena: A Partial Replication of the Haraldsson Findings", in PARAPSYCHOLOGY REVIEW, Mar-Apr. vol. 15(2), 13-15, 1984.

CHAPTER THREE
OBSESSION AND REINCARNATION

1. Jean Shinoda Bolen, GODDESSES IN EVERYWOMAN: A NEW PSYCHOLOGY OF WOMEN, New York, Harper & Row, 1984, p. 145.

2. Eleanor Cameron, THE WONDERFUL FLIGHT TO THE MUSHROOM PLANET, Boston, Little & Brown, 1954.

3. Sylvia Cranston and Carey Williams REINCARNATION: A NEW HORIZON IN SCIENCE, RELIGION AND SOCIETY, New York, Crown Pub., Inc., Julian Press, 1984, p. 293. According to Edgar Cayce the Akasha is the fundamental etheric substance of the universe, which retains the record of every sound, light, movement, or thought since its beginning.

4. Rabbi Yonassan Gershom, FROM ASHES TO HEALING: MYSTICAL ENCOUNTERS WITH THE HOLOCAUST, Virginia Beach, VA, A.R.E. Press, 1996, pp. 12-15.

5. Ian Stevenson, CHILDREN WHO REMEMBER PREVIOUS LIVES: A QUESTION OF REINCARNATION, Charlottesville, VA, Univ. Press of Virginia, 1987, p. 48.

6. Edith Fiore, THE UNQUIET DEAD, Garden City, NY, Doubleday & Co., Inc., 1987, p. 109.

7. Betty Riley, A VEIL TOO THIN: REINCARNATION OUT OF CONTROL, Malibu, CA, Valley of the Sun Publishing, 1984.

8. Ibid.

9. Ian Stevenson, Personal correspondence with the author, Charlottsville, VA, Nov. 1, 1994.

10. Ian Stevenson, CHILDREN WHO REMEMBER PREVIOUS LIVES: A QUESTION OF REINCARNATION, Charlottsville, VA, Univ. Press of Virginia, 1987, pp. 80-84.

11. Ian Stevenson, TWENTY CASES SUGGESTIVE OF REINCARNATION, (Second Edition), Charlottsville, VA, Univ. Press of Virginia, 1974, p. 357.

12. Jenny Cockell, ACROSS TIME AND DEATH: A MOTHER'S SEARCH FOR HER PAST LIFE CHILDREN, New York, Simon & Schuster, Fireside, 1994.

13. Ian Stevenson, TWENTY CASES SUGGESTIVE OF REINCARNATION, (Second Edition), Charlottsville, VA, Univ. Press of Virginia, 1974.

14. Morey Bernstein, THE SEARCH FOR BRIDEY MURPHY, new edition, New York, Doubleday, 1989.

15. Ian Stevenson, TWENTY CASES SUGGESTIVE OF REINCARNATION, (Second Edition), Charlottsville, VA, Univ. Press of Virginia, 1974, p. 223.

16. Morey Bernstein, THE SEARCH FOR BRIDEY MURPHY, new edition, New York, Doubleday, 1989, pp. 268, 123, and 165.

17. Betty Riley, A VEIL TOO THIN: REINCARNATION OUT OF CONTROL, Malibu, CA, Valley of the Sun Publishing, 1984.

18. Jenny Cockell, ACROSS TIME AND DEATH: A MOTHER'S SEARCH FOR HER PAST LIFE CHILDREN, New York, Simon & Schuster, Fireside, 1994.

19. Helen Wambach, RELIVING PAST LIVES: THE EVIDENCE UNDER HYPNOSIS, New York, Harper & Row, Pub., 1978, pp. 1-2.

20. Ibid, pp. 70-77.

21. Ibid, pp. 137-138.

22. Ibid, p. 3.

23. Ibid, pp. 115-116.

24. Ibid, p. 135.

25. Ibid, p. 140.

26. Raymond A. Moody Jr., COMING BACK: A PSYCHIATRIST EXPLORES PAST-LIFE JOURNEYS, New York, Bantam Books, 1991.

CHAPTER FOUR
HELGA, WHITE CLOUD, JOHN AND MARY

1. Leon E. Seltzer, ed. THE COLUMBIA LIPPINCOTT GAZETTEER OF THE WORLD, Morningside Hts., NY, Columbia U. Press, 1952, p. 652.

2. Germany, History of, ENCYCLOPAEDIA BRITANNICA, 15th ed., Macropaedia, 1976, vol. 8, p. 87.

3. Ibid, p. 86.

4. Ibid, p. 83.

5. Ibid, P. 84.

6. Kurt F. Reinhardt, THE RISE AND FALL OF THE "HOLY EMPIRE", Vol. 1 of GERMANY: 2000 YEARS, New York, Frederick Ungar Pub. Co., 1961, p. 158.

7. Germany, History of, ENCYCLOPAEDIA BRITANNICA, 15th ed., Macropaedia, 1976, vol. 8, pp. 83-84.

8. Ibid, p. 86.

9. Kurt F. Reinhardt, THE RISE AND FALL OF THE "HOLY EMPIRE", Vol. 1 of GERMANY: 2000 YEARS, New York, Frederick Ungar Pub. Co., 1961, p. 186.

10. Clark Wissler, INDIANS OF THE UNITED STATES, Garden City, NY, Doubleday & Co., Inc., 1966, p. 126.

11. Hiawatha, ENCYCLOPAEDIA BRITANNICA, 15th ed., Micropaedia, 1976, vol. V, p. 27.

12. Annick Hivert-Carthew (author of CADILLAC AND THE DAWN OF DETROIT, Davisburg, MI, Wilderness Adventure Books, 1994), Personal interview, May 10, 1993.

13. Ibid.

14. Graham Blackburn, THE ILLUSTRATED ENCYCLOPEDIA OF SHIPS, BOATS, VESSELS AND OTHER WATER-BORNE CRAFT, Woodstock, NY, Overlock Press, 1978, p. 96.

CHAPTER FIVE
SYNCHRONICITY IN FINDING AMANDA

1. C.J. Jung, SYNCHRONICITY: AN ACAUSAL CONNECTING PRINCIPLE, Princeton, NJ, Princeton Univ. Press, Bollingen Series, 1973, p. 103.

2. P.M.H. Atwater, COMING BACK TO LIFE: THE AFTER-EFFECTS OF THE NEAR-DEATH EXPERIENCE, New York, Ballantine Books, 1988, p.89.

3. Arthur Koestler, THE ROOTS OF COINCIDENCE, New York, Random House, 1972, p. 105.

4. Ibid, p. 106.

5. F. David Peat, SYNCHRONICITY: THE BRIDGE BETWEEN MATTER AND MIND, New York, Bantam Books, 1987, p. 17.

6. Marilyn Ferguson, THE AQUARIAN CONSPIRACY: PERSONAL AND SOCIAL TRANSFORMATION IN THE 1980'S, Los Angeles, J.P. Tarcher, Inc., 1980, p. 182.

7. F. David Peat, SYNCHRONICITY: THE BRIDGE BETWEEN MATTER AND MIND, New York, Bantam Books, 1987, p. 186.

8. Erich Segal, LOVE STORY, New York, Avon, 1970.

CHAPTER SIX
PSYCHIC READINGS, MOHARI, AND PSI

1. Doris Lessing, SHIKASTA: RE, COLONISED PLANET 5: PERSONAL, PSYCHOLOGICAL, HISTORICAL DOCUMENTS RELATING TO VISIT BY JOHOR (GEORGE SHERBAN) EMISSARY (GRADE 9) 87TH OF THE PERIOD OF THE LAST DAYS, New York, Knopf, 1979.

2. Richard Corriere and Joseph Hart, THE DREAM MAKERS: DISCOVERING YOUR BREAKTHROUGH DREAMS, New York, Funk and Wagnalls, 1977.

3. Sophy Burnham, A BOOK OF ANGELS: REFLECTIONS ON ANGELS PAST AND PRESENT AND TRUE STORIES OF HOW THEY TOUCH OUR LIVES, New York, Ballantine Books, 1990, p. 38.

4. Joseph Smith, translator, THE BOOK OF MORMON: AN ACCOUNT WRITTEN BY THE HAND OF MORMON UPON PLATES TAKEN FROM THE PLATES OF NEPHI, Salt Lake City, UT, The Church of Jesus Christ of the Latter-day Saints, 1978.

5. Jane Roberts, ADVENTURES IN CONSCIOUSNESS: AN INTRODUCTION TO ASPECT PSYCHOLOGY, New York, Bantam Books, 1979.

6. Julian Jaynes, THE ORIGIN OF CONSCIOUSNESS IN THE BREAKDOWN OF THE BICAMERAL MIND, Boston, Houghton Mifflin Co., 1990.

7. Jon Klimo, INVESTIGATIONS ON RECEIVING INFORMATION FROM PARANORMAL SOURCES, Los Angeles, Jeremy P. Tarcher, Inc., 1987, p. 28.

8. Foundation for Inner Peace, A COURSE IN MIRACLES, second ed., New York, Viking, 1996. This combined volume includes a workbook for students and a manual for teachers.

9. Lawrence Block, "Organic Writing", WRITER'S DIGEST, Sept. 1985, p. 55.

10. Andrew Neher, THE PSYCHOLOGY OF TRANSCENDENCE, Englewood Cliffs, NJ, Prentice Hall, Inc., 1990, pp. 197-198.

11. Lawrence Block, "Turnabout Is Fair Play", WRITER'S DIGEST, July 1987, pp. 47-48 & 50.

12. Carolyn Chute, THE BEANS OF EGYPT, MAINE, New York, Ticknor & Fields, 1985.

13. F. David Peat, SYNCHRONICITY: THE BRIDGE BETWEEN MATTER AND MIND, New York, Bantam Books, 1987, p. 194.

14. Fred Alan Wolf, PARALLEL UNIVERSES: THE SEARCH FOR OTHER WORLDS, New York, Simon & Schuster, 1988.

15. John Cornwell, THE HIDING PLACES OF GOD: A PERSONAL JOURNEY INTO THE WORLD OF RELIGIOUS VISIONS, HOLY OBJECTS AND MIRACLES, New York, Warner Books, 1991, p. 19.

16. Sam Keem and Anne Valley Fox, TELLING YOUR STORY: A GUIDE TO WHO YOU ARE AND WHO YOU CAN БE, New York, Doubleday, 1973, p. 143.

17. F. David Peat, SYNCHRONICITY: THE BRIDGE BETWEEN MATTER AND MIND, New York, Bantam Books, 1987, pp. 13-14.

18. Ibid.

19. J.E. Cirlot, A DICTIONARY OF SYMBOLS, London, Routledge & Kegan Paul, 1973, p. 84.

20. Stoker Hunt, OUIJA: THE MOST DANGEROUS GAME, New York, Harper & Row, Pub., 1985, p. 88.

21. Jon Klimo, CHANNELING: INVESTIGATIONS ON RECEIVING INFORMATION FROM PARANORMAL SOURCES, Los Angeles, Jeremy P. Tarcher Inc., 1987, p. 246.

22. Ibid, p. 279.

23. Kenneth Ring, HEADING TOWARD OMEGA: IN SEARCH OF THE MEANING OF THE NEAR-DEATH EXPERIENCE, New York, William Morrow & Co., Inc., 1984, pp. 221-227. According to Ring, near-death experiences are not the only routes to spiritual transformation. A dream could also serve as a catalyst.

24. Sophy Burnham, ANGEL LETTERS, New York, Ballantine Books, 1991.

CHAPTER SEVEN
SCIENCE AND DIVINATION

1. Roger Lewin, COMPLEXITY: LIFE AT THE EDGE OF CHAOS, New York, MacMillan Pub. Co., 1992, p.153.

2. Ibid, p. 154.

3. F. David Peat, SYNCHRONICITY: THE BRIDGE BETWEEN MATTER AND MIND, New York, Bantam Books, 1987, p. 40.

4. Ibid, pp. 51-52.

5. Fred Alan Wolf, PARALLEL UNIVERSES: THE SEARCH FOR OTHER WORLDS, New York, Simon & Schuster, 1988.

6. Douglas R. Hofstadter, METAMAGICAL THEMAS: QUESTING FOR THE ESSENCE OF MIND AND PATTERN, New York, Basic Books, Inc. Pub., 1985, p. 465.

7. Jane Roberts, ADVENTURES IN CONSCIOUSNESS: AN INTRODUCTION TO ASPECT PSYCHOLOGY, New York, Bantam Books, p. 122.

8. Marilyn Ferguson, THE AQUARIAN CONSPIRACY: PERSONAL AND SOCIAL TRANSFORMATION IN THE 1980's, Los Angeles, J.P. Tarcher, Inc., 1980.

9. Russel Targ and Harold Puthoff, MIND REACH: SCIENTISTS LOOK AT PSYCHIC ABILITY, New York, Delacorte Press, Eleanor Friede, 1977, p. 122.

10. Robert Jahn and Brenda Dunne, MARGINS OF REALITY: THE ROLE OF CONSCIOUSNESS IN THE PHYSICAL WORLD, New York, Harcourt Brace Jovanovich Pub., 1987.

11. Ibid, p. 201.

12. Ibid, p. 280.

13. P.M.H. Atwater, COMING BACK TO LIFE: THE AFTER-EFFECTS OF THE NEAR DEATH EXPERIENCE, New York, Ballantine Books, 1988, p. 14.

14. Ibid, p. 30.

15. Robert Jahn and Brenda Dunne, MARGINS OF REALITY: THE ROLE OF CONSCIOUSNESS IN THE PHYSICAL WORLD, New York, Harcourt Brace Jovanovich Pub., 1987, p. 142. (also see pp. 114, 313, and 258.)

16. F. David Peat, SYNCHRONICITY: THE BRIDGE BETWEEN MATTER AND MIND, New York, Bantam Books, 1987, pp. 181-182.

17. Ellin Dodge Young, YOU ARE YOUR FIRST NAME, New York, Pocket Books, Long Shadow Books, 1983, p. 1.

18. Walter B. Gibson and Litzka R. Gibson, THE COMPLETE ILLUSTRATED BOOK OF DIVINATION AND PROPHECY, Garden City, N.Y., Doubleday & Co., Inc., 1973, pp. 92-101.

19. Persi Diaconis and Frederick Mosteller, "Methods for Studying Coincidences", in J. OF THE AMER. STAT. ASSOC., vol. 84, No. 408, pp. 853-861, Applications & Case Studies, Dec. 1989, p. 860.

20. Theodore B. Dolmatch, ed. INFORMATION PLEASE ALMANAC 1981, New York, Simon & Schuster, 1980, p. 435.

21. Joseph F. Goodavage, WRITE YOUR OWN HOROSCOPE, New York, New American Library, Inc., Signet, 1975.

22. Astro Communications Services, Inc., ASTRO BASICS SERIES, San Diego, CA, Astro Communications Services, Inc., 1993, pp. 1-5. The report was prepared for the author on May 20, 1993.

23. Ibid, p. 4.

24. Malcolm Dean, THE ASTROLOGY GAME: THE INSIDE STORY: THE TRUTH ABOUT ASTROLOGY, New York, Beaufort Books, 1980, p. 281.

25. Michel Gauquelin, NEO-ASTROLOGY: A COPERNICAN REVOLUTION, London, The Penguin Group, Arkana, 1991, p. 23.

26. Percy Seymour, THE SCIENTIFIC BASIS OF ASTROLOGY: TUNING TO THE MUSIC OF THE PLANETS, New York, St. Martin's Press, 1992.

27. Michel Gauquelin, NEO-ASTROLOGY: A COPERNICAN REVOLUTION, London, The Penguin Group, Arkana, 1991, p. 171.

CHAPTER EIGHT
COLIN AND OTHER MIRACLES

1. Larry Dossy, RECOVERING THE SOUL: A SCIENTIFIC AND SPIRITUAL SEARCH, New York, Bantam Books, 1989, pp. 92 & 206. The forms and behavior of all biological systems are affected by organizing fields biologist Rupert Sheldrake calls morphogenetic. They allow thoughts to be connected across space and time.

2. Carlos Castaneda, THE TEACHINGS OF DON JUAN: A YAQUI WAY OF KNOWLEDGE, New York, Simon & Schuster, 1974.

3. Maggie Callanan and Patricia Kelley, FINAL GIFTS: UNDERSTANDING THE SPECIAL NEEDS AND COMMUNICATIONS OF THE DYING, New York, Simon & Schuster, Inc., Poseidon Press, 1992, p. 188.

CHAPTER NINE
THE TWO AMANDAS AND ME

1. Ian Stevenson, CHILDREN WHO REMEMBER PREVIOUS LIVES: A QUESTION OF REINCARNATION, Charlottsville, VA, Univ. Press of Virginia, 1987.

2. Jenny Cockell, ACROSS TIME AND DEATH: A MOTHER'S SEARCH FOR HER PAST LIFE CHILDREN, New York, Simon & Schuster, Fireside, 1994.

3. Ellin Dodge Young, YOU ARE YOUR FIRST NAME, New York, Pocket Books, Long Shadow Books, 1983, p. 3.

4. Ibid, p. 3.

5. Ian Stevenson, CHILDREN WHO REMEMBER PREVIOUS LIVES: A QUESTION OF REINCARNATION, Charlottsville, VA, Univ. Press of Virginia, 1987, p. 212.

6. Ibid.

7. Raymond A. Moody Jr., COMING BACK: A PSYCHIATRIST EXPLORES PAST-LIFE JOURNEYS, New York, Bantam Books, 1991, p. 37.

8. Barbara Ann Brennan, HANDS OF LIGHT: A GUIDE TO HEALING THROUGH THE HUMAN ENERGY FIELD, New York, Bantam Books, 1988, p. 64.

9. Caroll C. Calkins, ed., MYSTERIES OF THE UNEXPLAINED, Pleasantville, NY, The Reader's Digest Assoc., Inc., 1987, pp. pp. 300-301.

CHAPTER TEN
PAST LIVES AND SPIRITUAL GROWTH

1. Wade Clark Roof, A GENERATION OF SEEKERS: THE SPIRITUAL JOURNEYS OF THE BABY BOOM GENERATION, San Francisco, Harper San Francisco, 1993.

2. Sylvia Cranston and Carey Williams, REINCARNATION: A NEW HORIZON IN SCIENCE, RELIGION, AND SOCIETY, New York, Crown Pub, Inc., Julian Press, 1994, p. 222.

3. Jenny Cockell, ACROSS TIME AND DEATH: A MOTHER'S SEARCH FOR HER PAST LIFE

CHILDREN, New York, Simon & Schuster, Fireside, 1994.

4.   Brian L. Weiss, MANY LIVES, MANY MASTERS, New York, Simon & Schuster, Fireside, 1988.

5.   Kenneth Ring, HEADING TOWARD OMEGA: IN SEARCH OF THE MEANING OF THE NEAR-DEATH EXPERIENCE, New York, William Morrow & Co., Inc., 1984.

BIBLIOGRAPHY

The following references have been categorized to help the reader find materials. The placement may not reflect the essence of the book or article.

CREATIVITY

Adams, James L. THE CARE AND FEEDING OF IDEAS: A GUIDE TO ENCOURAGING CREATIVITY. Reading, MA: Addison-Wesley Pub. Co., Inc., 1986.

Aron, Arthur and Aron, Elaine N. "An Introduction to Maharishi's Theory of Creativity: the Empirical Base and Description of the Creative Process". THE JOURNAL OF CREATIVE BEHAVIOR 16(1): 29-49, 1982.

Braud, William and Jackson, Jan. "Psi Influence Upon Mental Imagery". PARAPSYCHOLOGY REVIEW 14(6): 13-15, 1983.

Bry, Adelaide. DIRECTING THE MOVIES OF YOUR MIND: VISUALIZATION FOR HEALTH AND INSIGHT. New York: Harper & Row Pub., 1978.

Cowling, W. Richard III. "Relationship of Mystical Experience, Differentiation, and Creativity". PERCEPTUAL AND MOTOR SKILLS. 61:451-456, 1985.

Greeley, Lillian. "The Bumper Effect Dynamic in the Creative Process: The Philosophical, Psychological and Neuropsychological Link". JOURNAL OF CREATIVE BEHAVIOR 20(4): 261-275, 1986.

Rose, Laura Hall. "A Model of the Creative Process Based on Quantum Physics and Vedic Science". THE JOURNAL OF CREATIVE BEHAVIOR 22(2): 139-153, 1988.

Suler, John R. "Primary Process Thinking and Creativity". PSYCHOLOGICAL BULLETIN 88(1): 144-165, 1980.

Taylor, Jeremy. DREAM WORK: TECHNIQUES FOR DISCOVERING THE CREATIVE POWER IN DREAMS. Ramsey, NJ: Paulist Press, 1983.

DREAMS

Corriere, Richard and Hart, Joseph. THE DREAM MAKERS: DISCOVERING YOUR BREAKTHROUGH DREAMS. New York: Funk and Wagnalls, 1977.

Freud, Sigmund. THE INTERPRETATION OF DREAMS. New York: Random House, Inc., Modern Library, 1978.

Scott, Susan S. "Dreams and Creativity in Women". THE ARTS IN PSYCHOTHERAPY 14: 293-299, 1987.

Sechrist, Elsie. DREAMS: YOUR MAGIC MIRROR. New York: Cowles Educ. Corp., 1968.

Wolman, Benjamin, ed.. HANDBOOK OF DREAMS: RESEARCH, THEORIES AND APPLICATIONS. New York: Van Nostrand, 1979.

DIVINATION

Astro Communications Services, Inc. ASTRO BASICS SERIES. San Diego, CA: Astro Communication Services, Inc., 1993.

Clow, Barbara Hand. UNDERSTANDING YOUR KEY LIFE PASSAGES: LIQUID LIGHT OF SEX. Santa Fe, NM: Bear & Company Pub., 1991.

Dean, Malcolm. THE ASTROLOGY GAME: THE INSIDE STORY: THE TRUTH ABOUT ASTROLOGY. New York: Beaufort Books, 1980.

Gauquelin, Michel. NEO-ASTROLOGY: A COPERNICAN REVOLUTION. London: The Penguin Group, Arkana, 1991.

Gibson, Walter B. and Gibson, Litzka R. THE COMPLETE ILLUSTRATED BOOK OF DIVINATION AND PROPHECY. Garden City, NY: Doubleday & Co., Inc., 1973.

Goodavage, Joseph F. WRITE YOUR OWN HOROSCOPE. New York: New American Library, Inc., Signet, 1975.

Seymour, Percy. THE SCIENTIFIC BASIS OF ASTROLOGY: TUNING TO THE MUSIC OF THE PLANETS. New York: St. Martin's Press, 1992.

Womack, David A. 12 SIGNS, 12 SONS: ASTROLOGY IN THE BIBLE, San Francisco: Harper & Row, 1978.

Young, Ellin Dodge. YOU ARE YOUR FIRST NAME. New York: Pocket Books, Long Shadow Books, 1983.

HISTORY

Baigent, Michael and Leigh, Richard. THE DEAD SEA SCROLLS DECEPTION. New York: Summit Books, 1991.

Bell, Susan Groag, ed.. WOMEN: FROM THE GREEKS TO THE FRENCH REVOLUTION. Stanford, CA: Stanford Univ. Press, 1973.

Bloch, Marc. SOCIAL CLASSES AND POLITICAL ORGANIZATION, Vol. 2 of FEUDAL SOCIETY. Chicago: Univ. of Chicago Press, 1971.

ENCYCLOPAEDIA BRITANNICA. "Germany, History of". 15th ed., Macropaedia, vol. 8, 1976: 69-126.

ENCYCLOPAEDIA BRITANNICA. "Hiawatha". 15th ed., Micropaedia, vol. V, 1976: 27.

Hivert-Carthew, Annick, author of CADILLAC AND THE DAWN OF DETROIT. Personal interview, May 10, 1993.

Reinhardt, Kurt F. THE RISE AND FALL OF THE "HOLY EMPIRE", Vol. 1 of GERMANY: 2000 YEARS. New York: Frederick Ungar Pub. Co., 1961.

Sabbagh, Antoine. EUROPE IN THE MIDDLE AGES. Englewood Cliffs, NJ: Silver Burdett Press, 1988.

Stubbs, William. GERMANY IN THE LATER MIDDLE AGES, 1200-1500. Arthur Hassall, ed., New York: Howard Fertig, 1969.

Waugh, Norah. CORSETS & CRINOLINES. London: B.T. Batsford LTD, 1954.

Wissler, Clark. INDIANS OF THE UNITED STATES. 1940. Rev. by Lucy Wales Kluckhohn, Garden City, N.Y.: Doubleday & Co., Inc., 1966.

HYPNOSIS

Anderson-Evangelista, Anita. HYPNOSIS: A JOURNEY INTO THE MIND. New York: Arco Pub., Inc., 1980.

Baker, Robert A. "The Effect of Suggestion on Past-Lives Regression". AMERICAN JOURNAL OF CLINICAL HYPNOSIS, 25(1):71-76, 1982.

Kihlstrom, John F. "Hypnosis". ANN. REV. PSYCHOL., 36:385-418, 385-418, 1985.

Laurence, Jean Roch; Nadon, Robert; Nogrady, Heather; and Perry, Campbell. "Duality, Dissociation, and Memory Creation in Highly Hypnotizable Subjects". INTERN. J. OF CLINICAL AND EXPER. HYPNOSIS, 34(4): 295-310, 1986.

Miller, Justin. "'Spontaneous' Age Regression: A Clinical Report". AMER. J. OF CLINICAL HYPNOSIS, 25(1): 53-55, 1983.

Schilder, Paul. THE NATURE OF HYPNOSIS. New York: Int'l. Univ. Press, Inc., 1956.

THE PARANORMAL

Atwater, P.M.H. COMING BACK TO LIFE: THE AFTER-EFFECTS OF THE NEAR DEATH EXPERIENCE. New York: Ballantine Books, 1988.

Block, Lawrence. "Organic Writing". WRITER'S DIGEST, Sept. 1985: 54-55.

Block, Lawrence. "Turnabout Is Fair Play". WRITER'S DIGEST, July 1987: 47-48, 50.

Brennan, Barbara Ann. HANDS OF LIGHT: A GUIDE TO HEALING THROUGH THE HUMAN ENERGY FIELD. New York: Bantam Books, 1988.

Bucke, Richard. COSMIC CONSCIOUSNESS. New York: E.P. Dutton, 1967.

Burnham, Sophy. A BOOK OF ANGELS: REFLECTIONS ON ANGELS PAST AND PRESENT AND TRUE STORIES OF HOW THEY TOUCH OUR LIVES. New York: Ballantine Books, 1990.

Burnham, Sophy. ANGEL LETTERS. New York: Ballantine Books, 1991.

Caldwell, Taylor. THE ROMANCE OF ATLANTIS. With Jess Stern. New York: William Morrow & Co., Inc., 1975.

Calkins, Caroll C., ed. MYSTERIES OF THE UNEXPLAINED. Pleasantville, NY: The Reader's Digest Assoc., Inc., 1987.

Castaneda, Carlos. THE TEACHINGS OF DON JUAN: A YAQUI WAY OF KNOWLEDGE. New York: Simon and Schuster, 1974.

Cornwell, John. THE HIDING PLACES OF GOD: A PERSONAL JOURNEY INTO THE WORLD OF RELIGIOUS VISIONS, HOLY OBJECTS AND MIRACLES. New York: Warner Books, 1991.

Dossey, Larry. RECOVERING THE SOUL: A SCIENTIFIC AND SPIRITUAL SEARCH. New York: Bantam Books, 1989.

Fiore, Edith. THE UNQUIET DEAD. Garden City, NJ: Doubleday & Co., Inc., 1987.

Foundation for Inner Peace. A COURSE IN MIRACLES, second ed. New York: Viking, 1996.

Geller, Uri. URI GELLER: MY STORY. New York: Praegar Pub., 1975.

Hunt, Stoker. OUIJA: THE MOST DANGEROUS GAME. New York: Harper & Row, Pub., 1985.

Ingram, Julia and Hardin, G.W. THE MESSENGERS: A TRUE STORY OF ANGELIC PRESENCE AND THE RETURN TO THE AGE OF MIRACLES. New York: Pocket Books, 1997.

Jahn, Robert and Dunne, Brenda. MARGINS OF REALITY: THE ROLE OF CONSCIOUSNESS IN THE PHYSICAL WORLD. New York: Harcourt Brace Jovanovich Pub., 1987.

Keem, Sam and Fox, Anne Valley. TELLING YOUR STORY: A GUIDE TO WHO YOU ARE AND WHO YOU CAN BE. New York: Doubleday, 1973.

Klimo, Jon. INVESTIGATIONS ON RECEIVING INFORMATION FROM PARANORMAL SOURCES. Los Angeles: Jeremy P. Tarcher, Inc., 1987.

Koestler, Arthur. THE ROOTS OF COINCIDENCE. New York: Random House, 1972.

Mack, John E. ABDUCTIONS: HUMAN ENCOUNTERS WITH ALIENS. New York: Charles Scribner's Sons, 1994.

Ring, Kenneth. HEADING TOWARD OMEGA: IN SEARCH OF THE MEANING OF THE NEAR-DEATH EXPERIENCE. New York: William Morrow and Co., Inc., 1984.

Roberts, Jane. ADVENTURES IN CONSCIOUSNESS: AN INTRODUCTION TO ASPECT PSYCHOLOGY. New York: Bantam Books, 1979.

Roberts, Jane. SETH SPEAKS: THE ETERNAL VALIDITY OF THE SOUL. Englewood Cliffs, NJ: Prentice-Hall, Inc., 1974.

Roberts, Jane. THE NATURE OF PERSONAL REALITY: A SETH BOOK. Englewood Cliffs, NJ: Prentice-Hall, Inc., 1976.

Stearn, Jess. THE SEARCH FOR A SOUL: TAYLOR CALDWELL'S PSYCHIC LIVES. New York: Fawcett Crest Books, 1973.

Strieber, Whitley. COMMUNION: A TRUE STORY. New York: William Morrow and Co., Inc., Beech Tree Books, 1987.

Strieber,Whitley. TRANSFORMATION: THE BREAK-THROUGH. New York: William Morrow and Co., Inc., Beech Tree Books, 1988.

Targ, Russel and Harary, Keith. THE MIND RACE: UNDERSTANDING AND USING PSYCHIC ABILITIES. New York: Villard Books, 1984.

Targ, Russel and Puthoff, Harold. MIND REACH: SCIENTISTS LOOK AT PSYCHIC ABILITY. New York: Delacorte Press, Eleanor Friede, 1977.

Walters, Ed and Walters, Frances. THE GULF BREEZE SIGHTINGS: THE MOST ASTOUNDING MULTIPLE SIGHTINGS OF UFOS IN U.S. HISTORY. New York: William Morrow and Co., Inc., 1990.

NATURAL SCIENCE

Bohm, David and Peat, F. David. SCIENCE, ORDER AND CREATIVITY. New York: Bantam Books, 1987.

Bower, Bruce. "Who's the Boss?" SCIENCE NEWS, April 26, 1986:266-267.

Davies, Paul. SUPERFORCE: THE SEARCH FOR A GRAND UNIFIED THEORY OF NATURE. New York: Simon and Schuster, 1984.

Diaconis, Persi and Mosteller, Frederick. "Methods for Studying Coincidences". J OF THE AMER. STATISTICAL ASSOC. 84(408):853-861, 1989.

Gleick, James. CHAOS: MAKING A NEW SCIENCE. New York: Viking, 1987.

Hofstadter, Douglas R.. METAMAGICAL THEMAS: QUESTING FOR THE ESSENCE OF MIND AND PATTERN. New York: Basic Books, Inc. Pub., 1985.

Levy, Steven. ARTIFICAL LIFE: THE QUEST FOR A NEW CREATION. New York: Pantheon Books, 1992.

Lewin, Roger. COMPLEXITY: LIFE AT THE EDGE OF CHAOS. New York: Macmillan Pub. Co., 1992.

Peat, F. David. SUPERSTRINGS AND THE SEARCH FOR THE THEORY OF EVERYTHING. Chicago: Contemporary Books, 1988.

Peat, F. David. SYNCHRONICITY: THE BRIDGE BETWEEN MATTER AND MIND. New York: Bantam Books, 1987.

Penrose, Roger. THE EMPEROR'S NEW MIND: CONCERNING COMPUTERS, MINDS, AND THE LAWS OF PHYSICS. Oxford: Oxford Univ. Press, 1989.

Rifkin, Jeremy. ENTROPY: A NEW WORLD VIEW. New York: Viking Press, 1980.

Thomsen, Dietrick E. "A High-Strung Theory". SCIENCE NEWS, Sept. 13, 1986:168-169.

Wolf, Fred Alan. PARALLEL UNIVERSES: IN SEARCH OF OTHER WORLDS. New York: Simon & Schuster, 1988.

PSYCHOLOGY

Blakeslee, Thomas R. THE RIGHT BRAIN: A NEW UNDERSTANDING OF THE UNCONSCIOUS MIND AND ITS CREATIVE POWERS. Garden City, NJ: Doubleday, Anchor Press, 1980.

Bolen, Jean Shinoda. GODDESSES IN EVERYWOMAN: A NEW PSYCHOLOGY OF WOMEN. New York: Harper & Row, 1984.

Brown, Barbara B. NEW MIND, NEW BODY: BIO-FEEDBACK: NEW DIRECTIONS FOR THE MIND. New York: Harper & Row, Pub., 1974.

Callanan, Maggie and Kelley, Patricia. FINAL GIFTS: UNDERSTANDING THE SPECIAL NEEDS AND COMMUNICATIONS OF THE DYING. New York Simon & Schuster, Inc., Poseidon Press, 1992.

Chopra, Deepak. QUANTUM HEALING: EXPLORING THE FRONTIERS OF MIND/BODY MEDICINE. New York: Bantam Books, 1989.

Chopra, Deepak. UNCONDITIONAL LIFE: MASTERING THE FORCES THAT SHAPE PERSONAL REALITY. New York: Bantam Books, 1991.

Ferguson, Marilyn. THE ACQUARIAN CONSPIRACY: PERSONAL AND SOCIAL TRANSFORMATION IN THE 1980's. Los Angeles: J.P. Tarcher, Inc., 1980.

Freud, Sigmund. THE INTREPRETATION OF DREAMS. New York: Random House Inc., Modern Library, 1978.

Green, Elmer and Green, Alyce. BEYOND BIOFEEDBACK. New York: Delacorte Press, 1982.

Jaynes, Julian. THE ORIGIN OF CONSCIOUSNESS IN THE BREAKDOWN OF THE BICAMERAL MIND. Boston: Houghton Mifflin Co., 1990.

Jung, C.G. MODERN MAN IN SEARCH OF A SOUL. New York: Harcourt Brace Jovanovich, Harvest, 1933.

Jung, C.G. PSYCHOLOGY AND RELIGION. New Haven: Yale Univ. Press, 1938.

Jung, C.G. SYNCHRONICITY: AN ACAUSAL CONNECTING PRINCIPLE. Princeton NJ: Princeton Univ. Press, Bollingen Series, 1973.

Jung, C.G. THE BASIC WRITINGS OF C.G. JUNG, Violet Staub de Laszlo, ed., New York: Random House, The Modern Library, 1959.

Jung, C.G. THE MODERN MYTH OF THINGS SEEN IN THE SKIES. New York: Harcourt, Brace & Co., 1959.

Neher, Andrew. THE PSYCHOLOGY OF TRAN-SCENDENCE. Englewood Cliffs, NJ: Prentice-Hall, 1980.

Pearce, Joseph Chilton. THE CRACK IN THE COSMIC EGG: CHALLENGING CONSTRUCTS OF MIND AND REALITY. New York: Julian Press, 1988.

Roof, Wade Clark. A GENERATION OF SEEKERS: THE SPIRITUAL JOURNEYS OF THE BABY BOOM GEN-ERATION. San Francisco: Harper San Francisco, 1993.

Sheehy, Gail. PASSAGES: PREDICTABLE CRISES IN ADULT LIFE. New York: E.P. Dutton, 1977.

Thalbourne, Michael A. "Some Correlates of Belief in Psychical Phenomena: A Partial Replication of the Haraldsson Findings". PARAPSYCHOLOGY REVIEW, 15(2):13-15, 1984.

REINCARNATION

Bernstein, Morey. THE SEARCH FOR BRIDEY MURPHY, new ed. New York: Doubleday, 1989.

Cerminara, Gina. MANY MANSIONS. New York: The New American Library, Inc., Signet, 1967.

Chadwick, Gloria. DISCOVERING YOUR PAST LIVES. Chicago: Contemporary Books, Inc., 1988.

Cockell, Jenny. ACROSS TIME AND DEATH: A MOTHER'S SEARCH FOR HER PAST LIFE CHILDREN. New York: Simon & Schuster, Fireside, 1994.

Cott, Jonathan. THE SEARCH FOR OMM SETY: REINCARNATION AND ETERNAL LOVE. Garden City, NY: Doubleday & Co., Inc., 1987.

Cranston, Sylvia and Williams, Carey. REINCARNATION: A NEW HORIZON IN SCIENCE, RELIGION, AND SOCIETY. New York: Crown Pub., Inc., Julian Press, 1994.

Gershom, Yonassan. FROM ASHES TO HEALING: MYSTICAL ENCOUNTERS WITH THE HOLOCAUST. Virginia Beach, VA: A.R.E. Press, 1996.

Grant, Joan. FAR MEMORY: THE AUTOBIOGRAPHY OF JOAN GRANT. New York: Harper & Brothers Pub., 1956.

Leek, Sybil. REINCARNATION: THE SECOND CHANCE New York: Stein and Day Pub., 1974.

Lenz, Frederick. LIFETIMES: TRUE ACCOUNTS OF REINCARNATION. New York: Ballantine Books, 1986.

Marzollo, Jean. "`Mommy, I'm Scared!'" PARENTS MAG., Jan. 1986: 67-69.

Montgomery, Ruth. HERE AND HEREAFTER. Greenwich, CT: Fawcell Pub., Inc., 1968.

Moody, Raymond A., Jr. COMING BACK: A PSYCHOLOGIST EXPLORES PAST-LIFE JOURNEYS. New York: Bantam Books, 1991.

Riley, Betty. A VEIL TOO THIN: REINCARNATION OUT OF CONTROL. Malibu, CA: Valley of the Sun Pub., 1984.

Stern, Jess. THE SEARCH FOR THE GIRL WITH THE BLUE EYES: A VENTURE INTO REINCARNATION. Garden City, NY: Doubleday & Co., Inc., 1968.

Stevenson, Ian. CHILDREN WHO REMEMBER PREVIOUS LIVES: A QUESTION OF REINCARNATION. Charlottesville, VA: Univ. Press of Virginia, 1987.

Stevenson, Ian. Personal Correspondence with the author. Charlottesville, VA, Nov. 1, 1994.

Stevenson, Ian. TWENTY CASES SUGGESTIVE OF REINCARNATION, Second ed. Charlottesville: Univ. Press of Virginia, 1974.

Wambach, Helen. RELIVING PAST LIVES: THE EVIDENCE UNDER HYPNOSIS. New York: Harper & Row Pub., 1978.

Weiss, Brian L. MANY LIVES, MANY MASTERS. New York: Simon & Schuster, Fireside, 1988.

Whitton, Joel L. and Fisher, Joe. LIFE BETWEEN LIFE: SCIENTIFIC EXPLORATIONS INTO THE VOID SEPARATING ONE INCARNATION FROM THE NEXT. New York: Doubleday & Co., Inc., 1986.

OTHER SOURCES

Blackburn, Graham. THE ILLUSTRATED ENCYCLO-PEDIA OF SHIPS, BOATS, VESSELS AND OTHER WATERBORNE CRAFT. Woodstock, NY: Overlock Press, 1978.

Cameron, Eleanor. THE WONDERFUL FLIGHT TO THE MUSHROOM PLANET. Boston: Little & Brown, 1954.

Chute, Carolyn. THE BEANS OF EGYPT, MAINE. New York: Ticknor & Fields, 1985.

Cirlot, J.E. A DICTIONARY OF SYMBOLS. London: Routledge & Kegan Paul, 1973.

Dolmatch, Theodore B., ed. INFORMATION PLEASE ALMANAC 1981. New York: Simon & Schuster, 1980.

Lessing, Doris. RE: COLONISED PLANET 5, SHIKASTA: PERSONAL, PSYCHOLOGICAL, HISTORICAL DOCUMENTS RELATING TO VISIT BY JOHOR (GEORGE SHERBAN) EMISSARY (GRADE 9) 87TH OF THE PERIOD OF THE LAST DAYS. New York: Knopf, 1979.

Segal, Erich. LOVE STORY. New York: Avon, 1970.

Seltzer, Leon E., ed. THE COLUMBIA LIPPINCOTT GAZETTEER OF THE WORLD. Morningside Hts., NY: Columbia U. Press, 1952.

Smith, Joseph, translator. THE BOOK OF MORMON: AN ACCOUNT WRITTEN BY THE HAND OF MORMON UPON PLATES TAKEN FROM THE PLATES OF NEPHI. Salt Lake City, UT: The Church of Jesus Christ of the Latter-day Saints, 1978.

About the Author

Ms. Gates holds a Master's degree in psychology and has taught at colleges and universities. For thirteen years she has led a writers' group. She is completing *JOURNEY INTO AZURE NIGHT*, a science fiction novel based on a past life obtained through hypnotic regressions.

Ms. Gates lives with her husband and teen-aged son in Michigan.